Purestrike™

The 5 Simple Keys to Consistency

ISBN 978-1-938653-06-3
Copyright © 2012 Pure Strike, LLC. All rights reserved. Pure Strike and the Pure Strike Keys are trademarks of Pure Strike, LLC.

The 5 Simple Keys to Consistency

Contents

Introducing PureStrike:
The 5 Simple Keys to Consistency *4*

The Swing: Chipping
Learning the 5 Keys Using the Smallest Motion First *48*

The Swing: Pitching
Learning the 5 Keys Using a Longer Motion *55*

The Swing: Full Swing
Learning the 5 Keys Using a Full Swing Motion *63*

Swing Speed: Maximizing Speed with the 5 Keys *66*

Educated Hands: The Secret to Clubface Control *76*

PureStrike: Drills for the 5 Keys *85*

PureStrike: Lessons *110*

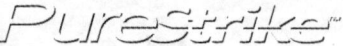

Introducing PureStrike:
The 5 Simple Keys to Consistency

BOB KOCH: Hello! I'm Bob Koch, President of Medicus Golf. You know, our only mission at Medicus is to help golfers improve and enjoy their golf game. After twenty years of research on the golf swing, with all the confusion and all the misunderstanding, we've taken and broken the golf swing down into five simple keys to allow you to understand and improve your golf game.

DAVE WEDZIK: For the last century the game's best players have actually exhibited very few things in common. There are however five distinct similarities that all great players do have in common. We call these the PureStrike keys. Until now these five simple keys have never been revealed together. These keys have been discovered by spending years studying the game's greatest players. Looking at these players in great detail has allowed us to conclude that using these five keys together is the simplest way to assure consistent PureStrike. The five simple keys are not only verifiable, but achievable by golfers of all levels, if they understand the fundamental movements and details behind each one. Let us take you through them now.

Key #1: Steady Head

Introduction

To maintain a Steady Head, you will note that as the backswing begins, the entire right side is stretching from the ankle, through the right knee and the right hip. In conjunction with this stretching, the left shoulder is moving the same degree, down and around. This movement allows the shoulders to turn at 90 degrees to the addressed spine angle and thus completes a centered shoulder turn. The Steady Head provides a reference point for this centered turn and provides the foundation for all remaining keys.

Key #2: Weight Forward

The average PGA Tour player arrives at impact with the great majority of their weight on the forward leg. The movement of the hips toward the target with the weight progressing forward is one of the most noticeable differences between the greatest and poorest players. It all works because of the proper sequence of motion; left knee, hips, shoulders, arms and club, get this sequence correct and you set the foundation for consistent ball striking.

Key #3: Flat Left Wrist

Maintaining a Flat Left Wrist is absolutely critical for a consistent pure strike. Having the Flat Left Wrist intact during impact is the most important alignment in golf. The left wrist must be flat and the club shaft in line with the left arm to strike the ball first before striking the ground.

Key #4: Sweetspot Path

The best golfers in the world have always understood that the game of golf is in no way played in a straight back and through manner. The golf club itself establishes that we play on an inclined plane and thus must swing the sweetspot down that inclined plane in a diagonal manner. When the sweetspot traces this path properly, it allows a golfer to strike the ball absolutely pure.

Introduction

Key #5: Clubface Control

Clubface Control is the ability to control the clubface relative to the Sweetspot Path to produce a shot that starts in a proper direction and curves as desired. Regardless of your chosen shot shape, proper clubface control allows a golfer to play the game with a predictable ball flight.

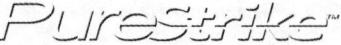

BK: Joining me today are two world-renowned golf instructors, world-renowned golf instructors, Chuck Evans and Dave Wedzik, and they're going to help me let you understand exactly how to learn these keys and enjoy your golf.

BK: Okay guys, we have these five keys. Now, where do you start?

CHUCK EVANS: Well, I think you have to start with a Steady Head, because you want to keep everything underneath, and having too much motion back and forth, which creates too much timing. So a Steady Head would allow you to have that motion, you know, without moving off the ball back and forth. So let's start with Steady Head.

Key #1: Steady Head

DW: If we were to play golf on this sort of horizontal plane, right, and look to keep our heads steady, it would be very simple for me to turn my shoulders in a circle right around that Steady Head, okay? Perfect! I can make that center shoulder turn from an extended upright position. We've got the ball down here on the ground, right? We're not playing in this standard upright position, we're bent over now.

CE: So a good swing thought would be not only stretch your right side in this backswing, but feel like your left shoulder is moving toward the left knee, and that will keep this all stretched out, so now you are stretching one side and actually what we would call compressing the other side.

DW: So Chuck, you're actually saying as you do this, you're actually saying that you're stretching this entire side in this direction.

CE: Yep! Everything is being stretched, while this is being compressed.

Introduction

BK: So let me make this simple. Let's say I have a club, and I start to rotate, at the same time I'm tilting, right?

CE: Yeah.

BK: Stretching, and that's what keeps me centered.

DW: Absolutely!

BK: Okay? So I have the stretcher talking about, right?

CE: Yeah!

BK: I'm right in the center, my head hasn't moved and I'm completely balanced.

CE: Right! So another way to do this, you stand in front of a mirror, like let's say the camera is the mirror, just put your club across your shoulders and stand up vertically, all right? And now, just turn your shoulders level, stand up straight, just turn your shoulders level, now bend forward.

DW: Right!

CE: There you go. It's pretty simple to do.

DW: That would be the simplest way to practice.

CE: That's the easiest way to practice it right there.

DW: Stand up straight. If I was to do that right next to Bob, I'd stand up straight, turn my shoulders level in a circle, and bend.

CE: And lean forward.

DW: That's it. And that's just -- that's the bend right down towards the golf ball.

BK: One other thing, when I was just doing that I felt my head still rotated, you know, it didn't stay totally, perfectly still, it actually rotated back, and as I went through it seemed to rotate forward.

CE: Well, your neck and head are going to rotate back and forward. What we ideally don't want to see though is the head moving side-to-side, nor great extent of up and down.

BK: You're saying that I really need to be able to pivot the right way to keep my head centered.

DW: Correct! It would be a proper pivot. And a great way to practice this would be, if you were just to stand there, and you were to go ahead and make backswings and if we had your head against a wall, you could just practice making backswings with your head staying right in its place, fixed on the wall there.

BK: Talking about the backswing, now we've got the downswing, does the head stay steady on the downswing?

DW: Absolutely, all the way to impact!

CE: If you stretched out your right side, compressed your left side, which kept your head say in a backswing, as you start down, as you shift your weight to the left and you're going to feel like you're moving your hips, knees, your whole weight's going left, as that's moving left, which is towards target, right, this way. That actually creates a side bend this way. So what I don't want to do is move my whole body left...

DW: And that's where his head would go forward.

10

Introduction

CE: So my weight stays -- my head stays right in the center, and as I push the hips and knees this direction, it makes my spine actually tilt that direction.

DW: Chuck, I'd like you to go ahead and show us again from the top as you start down. I want to explain here, Bob, again, one more time about what the axis tilt is on this downswing or what essentially is the side bend that happens on the other side. So you can see here as he pushes his hips forward, that's what's going to allow side bend for this side, right, this side bend, if I was to isolate that this way, it's going to allow this side bend to come in without Chuck having to actually manually, as he stated, move his head that way. As golfers we know we need that second, that bend, that side bend on the right side of the body, or that axis tilt, that's one of the big things that's going to help us launch the ball in the air. Okay? And so it's important that we're creating that with a Steady Head by sliding the hips forward, right, to keep the head steady and not by trying to create that tilt this way by simply manually...

CE: Right!

DW: ...Making it happen.

BK: So if the hips don't go forward and you side tilt back, you're going to --

CE: Yeah, I mean, if you're up here, and you don't move the hips forward and all you do is tilt this direction, the weight is on the back foot, you're going to chunk it, hit four feet behind the golf ball.

DW: So not only fat shots, thin shots too.

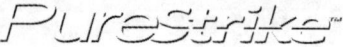

CE: Thin shots; fat and thin.

DW: Totally...

CE: And the only difference is, the only difference between those two is the club got down early to hit it fat, got down too early, but later it hit thin, okay, so it's the same shot.

DW: Mr. Smith got tired of slamming it in the ground 20 times in a row. And decided to go ahead and flip it more and pull the arms apart so he hit it thin.

CE: Right! So I mean, that's -- whatever you felt like in the backswing, you do the exact same thing in the downswing, except you're moving the Weight Forward as you start going through the stretch.

BK: I could be wrong, but I think the second key's the Weight Forward, isn't it?

CE: I think it is.

DW: Yeah, it is.

BK: Well, let's talk about that a little bit.

CE: Okay.

Key #2: Weight Forward

CE: So what we want to try to do is, once you get to the backswing, right, you kept your head steady. All right, so now from here, it's just like when I was pushing on your hip, and I do that because I don't want to get hit, all right? But right now what I'm going to do is you're going to feel your hips coming forward, while your head stays stationary, club is coming down on the golf ball. That's going to allow you to strike the ball first and then divot in front of it.

BK: Okay. So --

Introduction

CE: So at impact you're going to feel 70-85% of your weight on this left hip at impact.

DW: You're saying, Chuck, divot in front of that golf ball.

CE: Divot in front of the ball.

BK: So that's what you're talking about is getting that divot in front of the golf ball, by me, my weight transferring --

CE: To the left --

BK: -- to the left, that's going to allow me to hit the ball and then the ground.

CE: Yeah, it's going to steepen your angle coming into the golf ball.

BK: Well, why don't you guys show me how to do that?

DW: Absolutely!

CE: Dave, go ahead!

DW: So I'm going to strike this golf ball first and then the ground after and take a divot after the golf ball properly. From the top of my backswing, which is centered, I'm going to be moving my weight progressively forward onto my left leg, further and further as my hips go forward, and then continuously forward all the way to the finish. It looks something like this.

CE: Great divot! These are like the tour

divots. These are the ones that you want to see. You want to see that divot in front of that line.

BK: Well, that was the back of the ball where that line was,

CE: Right!

BK: So that divot is actually starting up --

CE: An inch-and-a-half in front of the golf ball.

BK: Right! And that happens because your weight's moving forward, your head is staying centered, and it's doing what?

CE: Well, with the Weight Forward, the head staying centered, it's allowing him to get his hands farther past the golf ball before the clubhead gets there.

DW: Keep that lean on that shaft.

CE: But there is another issue, a lot of people become ball-bound in this and they've got their eyes looking straight at that golf ball, and so a lot of times their hands want to quit and the club goes this way. So a good way to think about this is if you're in a bunker, a greenside bunker, you're not looking at the ball, you're looking at the spot where you want the club to enter the sand, which is behind the ball, because you're not trying to hit the ball, right? So in this case I would be looking at a spot an inch or inch-and-a-half in front of the golf ball. I wouldn't be looking at the ball during my swing; I'm looking where I want that club to strike the ground in front of the golf ball. So that allows me, also, I know that if I want to get the club up there, I know I've got to have more weight moving left in order to get to that point.

DW: So a different aiming point.

CE: Different aiming point, not ball, but in front of the ball. Okay?

BK: Okay. Let's see you hit one.

Introduction

CE: All right! So when I get set, again, all I'm trying to do is I'm looking up here.

DW: Nice!

CE: And my divot started right up in here.

BK: Yeah, yours actually started in front of his.

CE: Yeah. Well, I was looking at a point -- at the point in front of the ball and that's where I wanted the club to enter the ground. So again, a lot of this stuff you know subconsciously that if you're trying to move your hands farther this way, how are you going to get them there? You can't just do this, because your hands won't reach that point without all this breaking down. You know you've got to have more left, more left, more left, so that the hands can come more forward.

DW: You've got to have that weight, if you demonstrate that again, you've got to have that weight continuously moving forward.

CE: Continuously moving.

PGA Tour players average from 75-95% of weight/pressure forward at impact depending on the club used. Data compiled and verified by SwingCatalyst.

This example shows how the weight is moving throughout the swing as verified by Swing Catalyst. The resulting data is with all five keys

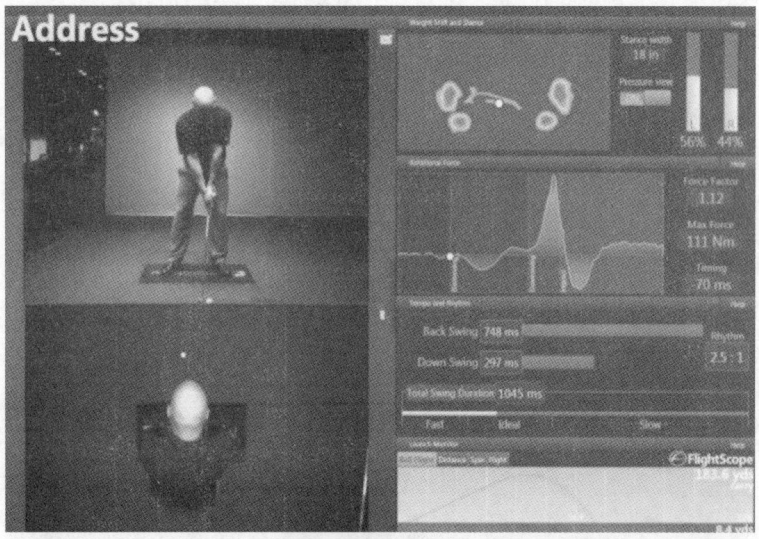

in place. You will note at address, my weight is 56% on my left leg. An acceptable range here is anywhere between a 50-50 split, all the way to 60% on the left leg.

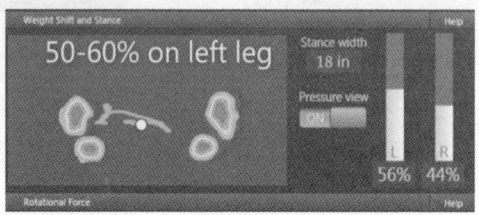

Introduction

As I reach the top of the backswing, the graph is showing a transfer which reaches 65% under my right leg. You can see from the photo that I have completed a centered 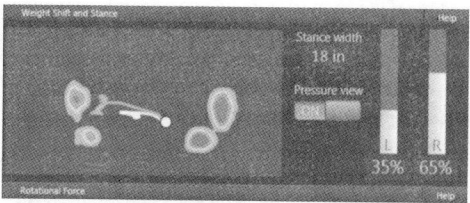 shoulder turn with a Steady Head however. This change is due to my

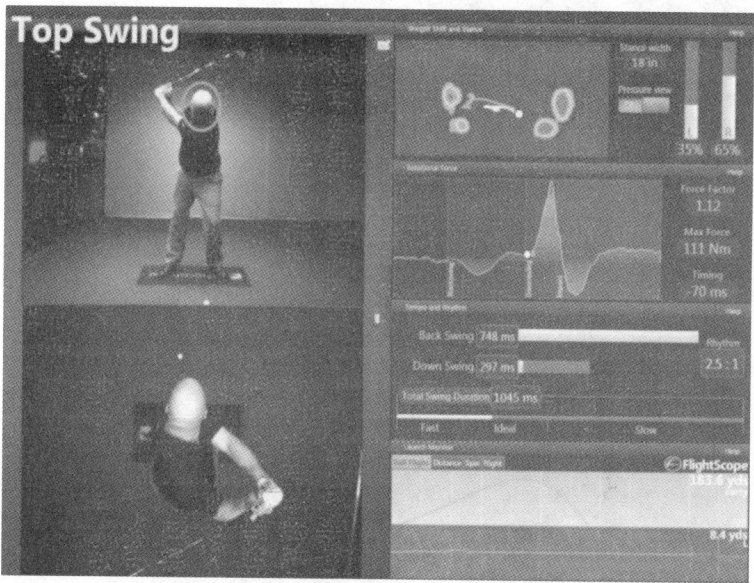

right leg straightening and the pressure I am adding to do so. By impact, you will note the massive shift forward of the weight initiated through the hip slide and added ground pressure. The left leg has now reached 87%, with only 13% on the right leg. The best golfers in the world achieve a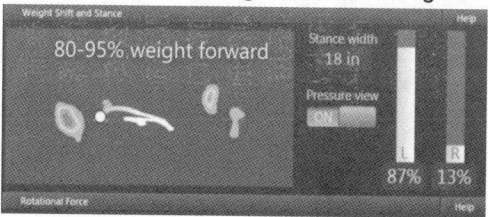

17

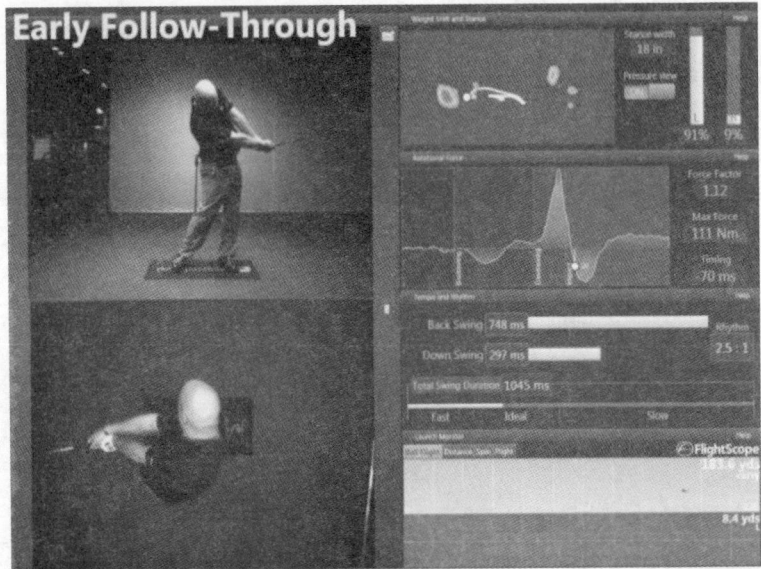

range of 80-95% Weight Forward while hitting an iron. Finally, early in the follow-through, the forward dimension has maxed out at 91%, showing that the weight has transferred progressively in that direction throughout the swing motion.

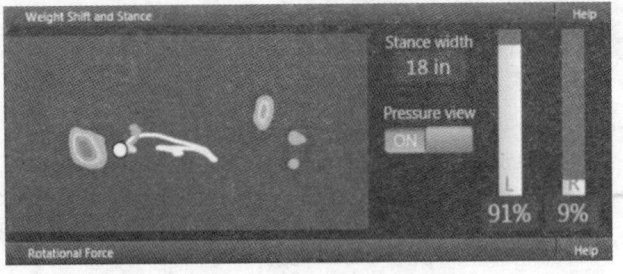

Introduction

BK: You know, okay, so, you know, I've tried to get my Weight Forward, I try, try, try, you know, sometimes it seems a little bit more difficult. You know, what happens if I don't get my Weight Forward?

CE: I mean, there's a lot of things that happen when you don't have your Weight Forward. You cannot hit down as deeply on the golf ball with the handle forward. You have a propensity to hang back, flip the club up this direction, you know, and you just can't produce as much power in hitting down on the golf ball. I'm going to have you put this little dowel here through your first two belt loops, even with your hips.

BK: All right! Let's figure this out.

DW: Then that Weight Forward, whether it's done properly or improperly, can dictate the path of the downswing.

CE: Go ahead and grab your club.

BK: Okay. All right!

CE: So let's say you go to the top. So now for your Weight Forward, you want to feel like your hips are sliding parallel to your target line. This will bring the club on the right path coming down into the golf ball. Some people, let's go to the top again, would slide their hips, what we will call cross-lateral, across the target line.

BK: Yeah.

CE: Now, see the club is going to get trapped up behind you, you're starting to stand up. Now you've got the path too much in to out.

DW: Shifting his hips that way, it's pulling the hips up underneath them, towards the golf ball, not towards the target, and it's shifting too much.

BK: I'm actually moving away.

CE: Right!

BK: You know, what's happening to my arms when my hips are moving forward?

DW: Well, if you go back and demonstrate this again real quick, we can take a look at that. So as you bring this up to the top, okay, and now as your hips start to move forward, your arms will stay connected better. Your left arm will start to slide down your chest, keeping the club, not only on playing, but approaching on the correct path. The easiest one to see is, again, if you're trying to move, instead of your hips going forward or sliding laterally towards the target, your hips are spinning too much and then backing up. Without forward you can see how much outward your left arm is shifting there.

BK: Almost missed the ball.

DW: Yeah. Your left arm is going to shift out. We see that all the time. People who are thinking that they should spin their hips to create some sort of power, the weight is not forward at all, in fact, it's almost backing up, and so they've got all the weight on their back leg at impact. And you see this as the handicap levels, as the handicaps get higher, we see

Introduction

a big propensity for the weight to be moving actually backwards.

CE: Go ahead and go up here again, and let's say that you start spinning the hips instead of sliding them, at this point your brain is going to go, I better hurry up and get to the golf ball, they're going to start throwing the club this way --

DW: Yeah --

CE: which now breaks down the left wrist. So instead of having a flat left wrist through the golf ball, you have a bent left wrist.

BK: Which if I'm correct, that is the third key, right?

CE: That is the third key.

Key #3: Flat Left Wrist

BK: Okay, Flat Left Wrist. What is a Flat Left Wrist? I mean, why do you have to have a Flat Left Wrist?

CE: Every one of these clubs has a design built into it. They all have what's called the Leading Edge and they all have what's called the Trailing Edge. So when I set that club down, like this, you can see how the grip end is farther in front than the face is, right? That's the design of the club. So if I made impact, just how the club is designed, my hands will look like this. That would give me the true loft of the club. If I allow the clubhead to go past my hands, now the shaft's

leaning back and I've added loft to it. So when you see a tour event they go, he's got a 196 yards, he's going to hit a 6-iron. Most people would love to hit a driver at 96 yards, right? They're actually taking that 7-iron or that 6-iron and they are de-lofting it even more. They're turning it into about a 4-iron, whereas the average person is taking that same 7-iron, and turning it into a 9. Dave!

DW: Well, this starts with -- we can start right with some of the other keys that we've already talked about; the stable head is allowing us to keep the weight, for your starting piece, to keep the Weight Forward, and I would say we can -- if I had to have you set up to this ball, Bob, you're going to be able to see that Weight Forward is one of the big controlling components, okay, to being able to establish Flat Left Wrist. So we talked about this before in one of the previous keys, if I take you up to the -- if you go up to the top of the backswing, okay, and if your weight was actually moving backwards, okay, this would be the biggest propensity to start to flip at the ball, okay, and hit the ball with the club, with this leading edge not on the ground anymore, and the feeling that you're going to try to add loft to lift that ball in the air. Okay? As opposed to, if we were to do this correctly, shifting from the top, shifting the Weight Forward, okay, allowing the hands to travel forward and longer, that would make it much simpler to have this club soled properly, and use the tool correctly there, okay, with this weight fully forward.

BK: Well, it actually feels like it's making my -- it's actually producing the left -- Flat Left Wrist by the path that it's coming down.

DW: Absolutely, it's definitely helping to produce it. And talking about the making of the

Introduction

divot in front of the golf ball with the Weight Forward and the Flat Left Wrist and doing this properly, let's go over the different wrist conditions, being flat or if the left wrist was bent, or the left wrist was even arched, and what that would do to divot location.

BK: Okay.

DW: So if you were to go ahead and set up and you were going to make a backswing and we had you make -- start down and you were to actually -- even with your Weight Forward, okay, you were to bend your left wrist prematurely or collapse it or flip it at the bottom, okay, this would move a low point further back, okay, and it will cause the club to enter the ground further back. So the club -- so the bent left wrist would have the club already traveling up as it reached the golf ball. And that's one of the -- it's one of the biggest problems we see, wouldn't you say, Chuck?

CE: Right!

DW: With amateur players all over, is that, that left wrist is actually bending prematurely due to a few different reasons.

CE: Yeah, I mean to a number of reasons, but that bent left wrist, I mean, any type of ball flight you can think of; fat, thin, high, low, left, and right, happens from that risk condition. That bending of that left wrist creates all those different ball flights, of which none of those you can play golf with. Go ahead and now talk about the arching.

DW: Okay, yeah. So conversely if you were to go ahead and you actually started to arch this left wrist, okay, into this condition, that would certainly move the handle further forward, okay? It would be further forward, but then the radius is actually destroyed in the other way, okay? It's not lining up in time, we're not getting this forearm and shaft in line by impact.

PureStrike

CE: And by arching that left wrist, it also changes your low point, because that arching now, that wrist becomes a low point. So if you had your ball play in this normal position, if you hit it, you'd hit low cuts. So you'd have to move the ball forward to compensate for that.

DW: Because you're moving your low point further forward with that arched wrist condition.

BK: I'm not sure I get that.

CE: All right! So let's say with a Flat Left Wrist that this position works really well. Now we're going to arch the left wrist. See how that also opens the face?

BK: Uh-huh.

CE: So now I would have to move this ball location up to there to get the same angle I had with the Flat Left Wrist. If I was coming in impact like this, I would have to move the ball back to here.

BK: To get this, so the face is square?

CE: Yes.

BK: Got it! Because that's actually shutting the face.

CE: Yes. So in a perfect world, you want to have a Flat Left Wrist, but if you're going to err on one side or the other, always err towards the arching or rounding off of the wrist, not to this one.

BK: Because of the fat shots.

CE: Right!

Introduction

DW: And the other side of that is too, going back to those, the arched wrist will be a component that would keep the club traveling into out the most, okay, whereas the bent left wrist would shift the path out to the innermost --

BK: The over the top --

CE: Right!

DW: -- which would lead to the most slices, the most over the top.

CE: Right!

BK: Okay, so that really is the master key of them all, it could potentially be, huh, is that this is how, with that key, this is what actually makes the ball go up in the air?

CE: Right, Flat Left Wrist, because it gives you more control of the clubface and the club shaft and helps in that angle of attack and going into the golf ball.

DW: It keeps that radius completely intact, right?

CE: Right!

DW: Keeps the forearm and the club shaft lined up so the club continues to travel down, so this golf ball can be struck, and struck first with a divot after the wall. I know, Chuck, we see students all the time and they've got the completely wrong idea with what it takes to get a golf ball in the air.

CE: Right!

DW: They've got the impression that they're seeing all that loft down there and they believe that they're -- and they want the ball to go high and they believe that they're going to actually bend the left wrist, keep their weight back, right, to lift the ball up in the air. I think it's important we're really clear on this, that that's not how you go about getting the golf

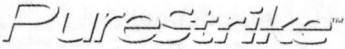

ball in the air properly. As you showed earlier, that would be the way to impart the least backspin on the ball and even possibly topspin, as we hit these balls along the ground.

CE: And the shortest distance.

DW: And the shortest distance. Absolutely!

CE: So if you want to hit it high and short, that would be the way to do it, right?

DW: Right! And you'd be destroying this radius the fastest by bending that left wrist. I think what's important for -- and even if I've got -- I've got a 60 degree wedge here, which obviously has plenty of loft on it, we're going back to the way the clubs are built and how this leading and trailing edge have to rest on the ground. You can see how much that -- the look there is that this is very much de-lofted.

CE: I mean, that's -- severely --

DW: Very much forward.

CE: -- that handle was way in front of that clubface.

DW: Okay! Which if I was to put this then back in my hands, that would be a Flat Left Wrist

CE: -- In line.

DW: Or the inline lever condition right here.

CE: Right!

DW: Okay. So even if I'm hitting a 60 degree wedge, I'm still going to go ahead and hit the ball with the left wrist flat, the club still descending, like

Introduction

you explained earlier. So that ball can backspin up the clubface rather than trying to look at this club as if I'm trying to get the ball in the air and actually trying to lift it.

BK: Right.

CE: Right!

DW: I need to understand that I do need to hit down on the golf ball with my Weight Forward and that Flat Left Wrist.

CE: Right! And if you do that again, Dave, just go to the top, and as you start down, let's say I pushed your weight to the back, and now you start moving the club down. Well, that in itself is going to allow this clubhead to start passing the hands before it gets to the ball.

DW: Otherwise I can't hit the ball.

CE: But if he left his hands there and moved over here, that changes the relationship between the hands, club, and the body. So that's a big key in how your weight is moving to keep your hands forward, to lean the shaft forward, to hit down on the golf ball, to impart the backspin that gives it the lift to go.

BK: So these kind of go in order for a reason.

CE: Yeah.

DW: You know what that feels like to me, that feels when I do that, right, and when we go through that, that feels like I'm making very minimal compensations in my hands and wrists, and I've got all kinds of time to do it, rather than trying to make these maximum compensations of some sort in a very minimal amount of time. I think the Flat Left Wrist is a much simpler way to go about this.

CE: A lot simpler way. And again, once you get the hang of it, you understand that all you're trying to do is to take loft off the club.

DW: Absolutely!

CE: Then you'll be on your way towards the Flat Left Wrist.

DW: Be a great sensation for a lot of people, actually try to reduce loft, try to hit a 60 degree wedge at 40 degrees of loft.

CE: Right, and start to see divots in front of the golf ball, you know, and the more loft you have, is going to be.

DW: You want to throw me over a ball here, I'll hit one with a 60 degree wedge.

CE: I might add one more thing while you're setting up, Dave. So as he comes down into the golf ball at impact, if we can get the hands underneath the left shoulder, he can now throw this club as hard as he wants this way, but he's going to wind up striking the ball first before he does that. If his hands are back here and he starts moving the club, because his weight's not far enough forward, then he's going to hit it fat or thin back here. So the more weight you have forward, the more your hands are forward, if you push that as hard as you want with your right hand, you still can't throw it out of line before you get the golf ball and before the golf ball takes off.

DW: So I could really simplify this even a little further here and say, to

Introduction

make sure I hit that golf ball in the ground or take divots off to the golf ball, I've really got two things I really have to concentrate on: keeping my Weight Forward and having the Flat Left Wrist.

CE: Yeah.

BK: It's pretty good there!

CE: All right! So just like your irons and your wedges, the 3-wood also when soled properly, you can see that the grip is in front of the clubface. Now, it's not as much as a wedge, because this is a longer club, has less loft, but what that still means is that shaft is still going to be leaning forward at impact, just not as much as say a 60 degree wedge. So you're still hitting down, and you would still take a divot with your 3-wood or your hybrid. So anytime you're hitting a ball before that line, there's still a downward motion to it.

DW: Chuck, would you say talking about taking a divot with the 3-wood, would you say even if it's not a very pronounced divot, if the ball is laying down on the ground, there is still -- the club is still striking the ground, maybe a small divot, but that club is still striking the ground?

CE: Right, because it's closer up here to this, what we call straight line condition, because it's closer, that means it will be less down, the divot will be not as deep, and it won't be as long as a ball, let's say, positioned in the middle of your sternum.

DW: Perfect! Makes a lot of sense.

Key #4: Diagonal Sweet Spot Path

BK: Okay. So now we're on our fourth key. What's that key?

CE: That's called the Sweetspot Path. So by definition what we're trying to do is control the sweetspot, which is center of the clubface, and we want to control it through trailing our hands and feel pressure against this right index finger. So we're going to actually be directing our right index finger to control the sweetspot. The path of it of course is, was the path coming in the golf ball? And there's a couple of very simple things that we can show to give, you know, the viewers a feel for what happens on that Sweetspot Path.

DW: Best way to explain this would be to tell you that if we were to set up and put these two dowels out like this, this would be like parallel to the floor, okay? So this would be a horizontal plane. We're not playing baseball though, so we're not playing golf on this horizontal plane. If I was to flip these dowels perpendicular like this, we'd put them, they look like a wall. So now we'd be playing on a perfectly vertical plane. Think of croquet. But we're not playing croquet either, right, we're not making a stroke that looks something like this [makes vertical stroke], and we're not making a stroke that looks something like this [makes horizontal stroke]. We're making a stroke with a golf club. If  I get this club back, again, talking about the tool we use, right, clubs are bent. That dictates the fact that we play on an inclined plane. Okay? So not horizontal, not vertical, but inclined, okay, and that's what these shafts represent down here in the ground. And I was going to actually show you an exercise here, Bob. You stand over here as if you're addressing that golf ball, okay? I'm going to actually give you this hammer.

BK: Okay.

DW: Rubber mallet, okay, I'll take your club. And I'm going to set up this shaft to represent a stake in the ground, I'll go ahead and remove this, okay?

30

Introduction

BK: So that's -- again, that's on the same angle as the shaft.

DW: And that's representing the down, out, and forward downswing of the inclined plane.

BK: Okay.

DW: And I were to ask you to go ahead and set up, put the hammer at the back of that --

BK: Okay --

DW: and your only objective or your only instruction was to swing this back and drive that stake back into the ground, this is as simple as possible, if you had to drive that stake right back down into the ground, I want to see -- I'd like to see your backstroke.

BK: What I would do is take the hammer back --

DW: Yeah --

BK: and then I'd hit the --

DW: Okay, perfect! And that's exactly what you should do. And what you would note is that you would see that your hand and the hammer are drawing straight back, up, and in, right along the inclined plane. And I'll ask you, did you have any instinct to take that hammer out to the outside and drop it in the slot?

BK: No, not at all.

DW: No, none whatsoever.

BK: I knew that I needed to take it right up here and --

31

Purestrike

DW: Because it's the simplest way, right? It's the most efficient way.

BK: Right, absolutely!

CE: And it's not moving straight back along the target line either, is it?

BK: No, no, it's actually going in.

DW: Right! It's going -- it has three dimensions, it's going back, up, and in.

BK: But that's the optical illusion, it's -- you know, when I look at a straight target line, this isn't -- this isn't my target line.

DW: Exactly!

BK: This is actually going inside my target line.

DW: Exactly!

CE: That's a Sweetspot Path that it's traveling on.

BK: So on the inclined plane what you're saying is there is a straight line to the target line, but there is a line coming inside that, that it is the Sweetspot Path.

CE: Correct! So if we lay just this club down, where this is at, you'll see that this is actually the target line.

BK: Okay.

CE: We had those shafts laid up.

BK: Right!

Introduction

CE: So you see, you didn't take that club, that mallet along this line.

BK: No, I took it inside.

CE: You took it inside.

BK: Right!

CE: And then you brought it back down from the inside.

BK: Right!

CE: And as you go all the way down, let's say, through the golf ball, now because the hips are forward, the weight is forward, as you come through the golf ball, now you're going to go back, up, and in on the other side.

BK: Right! Well, it's really kind of funny is it actually made me feel like I was in that Flat Left Wrist condition that we talked about earlier.

DW: Absolutely!

BK: You know, when I came down the club was actually following from the inside and I actually had that bend in my right hand which was --

DW: Absolutely! Radius intact, down, out, and forward. The entire time.

BK: Got it!

CE: Having that bend in the right hand keeps that left wrist flat. And let's say that this was the -- let's say, it was the arc this way.

BK: Okay.

CE: And go ahead and grab your club, Bob.

BK: I don't know if I should have a hammer, a club or --

CE: And let's say your club is on that side of that circle.

BK: This side?

CE: Yeah.

BK: Okay.

CE: So now as you take that back.

BK: Okay.

CE: You're going to see how that moves -- starts moving inside.

BK: Right, I'm following that it's moving inside.

CE: Right! So as you get to the top --

BK: Okay --

Introduction

CE: what happens is, if your hips slide, like we talked about, more cross-lateral in this direction, you've actually shifted this line way to the right, your Sweetspot Path way to the right. So if I'm swinging now way to the right, what am I going to have to do to the clubface?

BK: Well, to get it at the target line I'm going to have to close it.

CE: Correct! So that's part of what's called Clubface Control, which we're going to talk about. That's another key.

BK: Okay.

CE: So let's say you go to the top again.

BK: Okay.

CE: But this time you spin your hips and you turn your chest. Now your circle is tilted this direction.

BK: Right!

CE: So now, how am I going to get that shot back?

BK: I'm going to have to open the face so that it doesn't go left.

CE: Right! So you're going to have to open the face again. So again, you're changing the angle of that sweetspot, and in both of those cases now you have to manually try to control the sweetspot with clubface control, right, to get this curve back to target.

DW: I think what's key to note in both of those is that the weight is not going forward.

BK: Right!

CE: Right!

DW: Your weight is either shifting out towards the golf ball or it's rotating and shifting back too much.

CE: Got it!

DW: So the weight is not going forward with both of those options.

CE: So what we're saying is, if you didn't do any of those and you just took that up, just like you did with that hammer, and now you slid down here parallel to the target line, towards the target, you don't have to manipulate any of it and you're controlling your sweetspot perfectly.

BK: Okay. So let's finally get this straight. Now, this is the target line, right?

CE: Uh-huh.

BK: Now, I'm supposed to swing my club down this target line to hit the ball down the target line, right, correct?

CE: No. You'd only swing down the target line if you wanted to hit it short, because as we discussed earlier, we don't play golf on a vertical plane, we play golf on a slant. So that's why when you get that thing with the hammer, the sweetspot is coming from inside the golf ball. It's hitting the inside part of the golf ball. It's not hitting the back of the ball, nor the outside of the golf ball, but that's a mistake a lot of people make. They think they have to swing the club down this target line. Dave, why don't you demonstrate what it would look like, a swing that is going along target line versus a swing that's going too much in --

DW: Absolutely!

CE: -- and how that affects Sweetspot Path and Flat Left Wrist and all that stuff.

Introduction

DW: Yeah, absolutely! And I would say, Bob, as Chuck kind of explained what I'm doing here, I would say that the reason people do it that way is, they picture, their eyes can see this extended target line and their mind is telling them to try to swing down that line, but again, remember, we talked about this already, this is not a vertical plane we play on, so we can't make our stroke in this manner. We're playing on an inclined plane and that sets up the proper down, out, and forward path. So I'll go ahead and I'll demonstrate. So if I was to take a swing here and keep the sweetspot actually tracing this target line, it would look something like this. It's hard to do guys. I'm struggling here. I don't feel like I can hit the ball very far like that.

CE: So it's not a very golf like motion, would you say?

DW: It feels very non-golf like.

CE: So it's almost -- it's almost Jim Furykish in the backswing.

DW: Absolutely! With no shift.

CE: Yeah. With no shift. And then you've got the other person that drags it way in.

DW: Right, they've been told maybe to take their hands inside or swing to the inside, right?

CE: And now they think they're too far back, so again, they try to move the sweetspot out to swing down the target line. So now here's what's happening. The left wrist is starting to bend down. So again, they can't get the ball started online.

DW: So I've completely lofted the Flat Left Wrist, because it's the only way-- by bending that wrist is the only way I can keep the club tracing that target line.

CE: Right!

DW: Okay? So done correctly for the proper inclined plane, as a golfer I need to understand that I not only take my hands inward and the clubhead inward, but that I go ahead then, and as my hips push forward, okay, one of the keys, I'm going to drive my hands straight down, out, and forward, all the way to that golf ball and through.

CE: Now, when you're driving your hands, is there a certain spot that you focus on? You know, we call it, you know, your Club Head Control on what you're focusing on.

DW: Definitely!

CE: Can we cover that?

DW: Good question! Yeah. I'm basically going ahead, I'm trying -- the joint here, this third joint up here in the index finger, in the right index finger, I'm keeping pressure on the shaft the entire time to maintain and keep driving that sweetspot with the pressure right down that -- down, out, and forward, right down that visual equivalent of this line to me, okay, right down that line that I can see now tracing, continuing to go down, out, and forward. One of the things you can do, actually, Bob, if you'd step in here for a second, I want to kind of show you a good way to feel that sweetspot pressure as we start to drive it down that line. If you go ahead and take that club back, if you're going to go ahead

Introduction

and keep driving your hands straight down, out, and forward, on that angle that we just talked about, out towards the golf ball, all the whole time maintaining this pressure here, and I'm going to go ahead and put a little bit of pressure back and you really feel that now, right?

BK: Oh yeah!

DW: You can really feel all that pressure building up here --

BK: Right!

DW: -- right? And there is going to be a ton of speed created right down at the golf ball.

BK: Right!

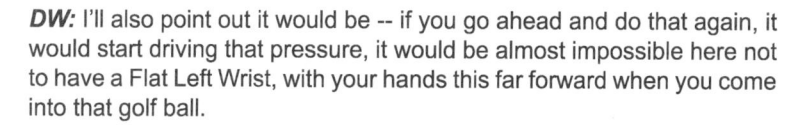

DW: I'll also point out it would be -- if you go ahead and do that again, I would start driving that pressure, it would be almost impossible here not to have a Flat Left Wrist, with your hands this far forward when you come into that golf ball.

CE: So if you want to hit the ball towards target, you can't swing along target line. It's just a reference point for us to set up to.

BK: Okay. So what's the bottom line?

DW: Yeah, so let's talk about how simple this really is and let's tie in the other keys we've talked about up till now to really get down to how easy it is to have this sweetspot, all right, going down the proper path, on the Sweetspot Path.

BK: Okay.

DW: So if we go right back to the beginning, we talked about stable head, I want to make a very simple centered shoulder turn around that stable head, I'm going to have my hands tracing back, up, and in, directly up the inclined plane, setting me up for a perfect downswing. Going back to another one of the keys, Weight Forward, I'll start to slide my hips forward towards the target, that's moving the Weight Forward. As long as I maintain this Flat Left Wrist, I'm driving right down that straight line delivery path, which is the visual that I see from my eyes, right through to finish. Sweetspot, tracing the proper path down the inclined plane the entire time.

BK: I've got a question for you. When you were just bringing that club down, it looked like you were actually coming from the inside and you are going to hit across that now to the right.

DW: That's interesting you say that, because to my eyes it really does look like that, okay, and that's going to lead us into this fifth key, which is Clubface Control, and I think that's what we talk about next.

CE: Right!

BK: Okay.

Key #5: Clubface Control

BK: Okay. Now, I need to understand how I'm going to swing on this Sweetspot Path if this is my target line, right?

CE: Uh-huh.

BK: Okay, let's say we set it up and that's the ball and that's the target, the Sweetspot Path, and I'm swinging on that path and that's my target line, I need to understand how I'm going to hit that ball straight at my target if I'm swinging on that Sweetspot Path? To me, it looks like I'm going to hit it way out to the right.

DW: Is your question how you would go ahead and hit a dead straight shot right at your target?

Introduction

BK: Ultimately I want to get the ball at the target.

DW: Okay.

CE: Okay. So Dave, how many players you see on tour who hit the ball dead straight?

DW: Yeah, I would say that if you want to play the toughest possible shot you could play, you'd go for the dead straight shot, and I can think of nobody currently playing the tour at the highest level of golf in the world that's playing a dead straight golf shot. Everyone's playing a shot with some curvature.

CE: So they all have curvature to their shots.

DW: They're all putting curvature.

CE: So the way that we have this set up that we've gone through so far in the five keys, the shot that we have set up is for you to hit what would be called a push draw. The ball starts slightly right at target and then draws back towards target. And then we can also show you how to hit the fade, the ball starts slightly left and then curves back to it. A straight shot is a harder shot to hit. It can be done obviously, but there's a reason why the world's best players don't play that shot, they're playing a shot to always work toward the target.

BK: Absolutely!

CE: So we set it up this way to show you how to do it hitting a push draw.

BK: All right.

CE: So let's do that.

BK: Could you show us?

DW: Yeah, absolutely! So we can see this -- we've got the white line, the delivery line, that motion of driving the hands down, out, and forward on the down stroke, and what we started to discuss was to dictate the start line, we have to know where the clubface is pointing when it hits it. So if what I'm showing here with this tool I've got on the club is that this clubface is pointing left where it's closed to this path right here, that is going to impart draw spin on this golf ball and effectively work that ball back towards the intended target. Okay, that's how we're getting this shot that we're swinging out to this degree to curve back to the intended target. Okay? If this face was actually more open and it matched that line, that would be a ball that started exactly on that path and stayed there. So it would be a straight push, it would be a ball that never came back. Those two things match, the ball never comes back. Okay? We took this to a further degree and changed that face angle to show that the face angle is aiming more left or more closed to that path, that ball would start where the face is pointing, okay, and it would curve because of the differential of the path to the face, it would have even bigger curve to the left. So this would be almost a hook at that point, the ball that would start out and take a bigger curve to the left.

BK: So the more the differential between the path and the face, the more --

CE: The bigger the curve.

DW: Exactly!

BK: Okay.

DW: Bigger the differential, bigger the curve. So if I was to turn this face well closed to that path, this ball would be what someone might describe as a snap hook. So really what we're looking for is a face angle that is just slightly closed to that path, again, maybe only a couple of degrees,

Introduction

and that's going to make the ball just curve gently back to the target. Okay?

BK: Well, my question is, okay, so how do we control the face to the path?

CE: And you do that through what we'd call educating your hands, and so your hands have to make a certain motion. Once you take your grip, wherever your hand goes, the clubface wants to follow it. So if I don't have educated hands, I don't know where this club is going, I can do it another way. I can preset my clubface angle to the curve I want to hit, to my path, and then swing the club back and down without changing it, and that will do the same thing. Or I can train myself how to take this club, for instance, and make little motions to go like this, or like this, or whatever I'm trying to hit with the shot, I just train my hands to make that particular motion.

DW: So whether you want to have the clubface more closed or more open.

CE: More closed or more open, which is going to change your trajectory. And then I saw, in fact, just the other day, I saw a guy on TV, famous announcer, blonde-headed guy, shot 63 in the US Open one year, he was talking about, he was doing his clinic, he was talking about, this is a great way for people to train their hands. He said, go ahead and set up to your ball, make a backswing, come down, stop at the ball, is the face square? If you want it more closed, make it more closed. If you want it more open, make it more open. But make a swing, come down to the ball, stop it and see where the face is. That was his way of getting people to educate their hands. So you know, how we do it obviously is we start with the smallest shots in hand education, with chipping, move to pitching, and then into full swing. Learn how to control the clubface via these hands. So if I learn how to control the hands, I can control the face. If I can control the face, I can control the ball. If I can control the ball, then I control where it's going out to target. So it all starts with educating the hands.

DW: So if I understand this right, Chuck, if you were going to hit a draw and you were just going to do it by having it be dictated by what you set up, you would know approximately where you were going to -- what your intended path was going to be for the downswing, and you would just set your face slightly close to that.

CE: Slightly close to that path.

DW: You are going to hit a draw, and if you were going to hit a fade, it would be vice versa, you'd set that slightly open to that.

CE: Yeah, except, also, if we're going to hit a fade, we have to change all of our lines, because we'd have to move our lines to the left of target so I can fade back. But you would still do the same thing, the same exact thing.

DW: So you could just simply shift your alignment to the left --

CE: Right, to the left --

DW: -- so the ball could start left.

CE: And then you have your face slightly open to the path. So now you've got ball starts left, curves back to target. If you want to hit the draw, the ball is going to start right, with slightly closed face to the path, then it's going to draw back to the left. So you do that by matching face and path to get the desired amount of curvature that you want.

DW: So in a nutshell, you aim a little more left for a fade and a little more right for a draw.

CE: Yeah.

Introduction

DW: Okay. Straight push, face aiming right, Sweetspot Path, more to the right, ball position slightly back.

Okay. Push, then draws back slightly, shouldn't over curve, face will be closed to the path, but aiming, pointing right of intended target at impact. Biggest push with draw, ball furthest back, face most to the right, most closed to the path.

Some balls will start left now, so I'm shifting my alignments, moving baseline, more left, ball not so far back. This is going to be a straight pull, face aiming left, matching the path. Straight pull.

First time we'll bring fade spin in. So this is the first time we're going to have a face that's actually open to the path. Alignments and baseline are still left, face just open to the intended path, curving back.

Straight shot, face and path match. Pretty good!

Introduction

BK: Okay. If we wanted a one-minute PureStrike lesson --

CE: Okay.

BK: Let's see it.

DW: I would say that if we were going to go through a one-minute PureStrike in how to do this correctly, we'd start going through the keys, understand that we need a Steady Head. I'm going to go ahead, thought process is to make a centered shoulder turn around that Steady Head as a post. Hands are going inward, making sure we start to put together the proper path, or the proper back, up, and in for the inclined plane. For the start down, the key is to move the Weight Forward, very simple, just keep the weight moving target-ward. That's going to help me maintain the Flat Left Wrist, help me maintain the radius. Okay? From there, we're simply going to keep the head steady by moving the hips forward, and then through proper training in educated hands, make sure we understand that if we are swinging slightly down, out, and forward, the face needs to be slightly closed to that path to hit the proper push draw.

BK: That sounds simple.

DW: I'd say very simple.

CE: So in addition to that, when you move your hips forward, that's also going to help bring the club down that Sweetspot Path we talked about.

DW: Yeah.

CE: All right, so those five keys all put together, you master those, and this is a pretty simple game.

DW: Can get a lot easier for lots of people.

CE: Yeah.

The Swing: Chipping
Learning the 5 Keys Using the Smallest Motion First

CHUCK EVANS: The best way to learn is to start with a shorter shot, because if you can't control those keys within about a two foot area, how are you going to control it from the top of the swing of the driver?

BOB KOCH: That's a good point.

CE: Right? So we start with chipping, and we go through the keys and how they apply to chipping, and how you apply them to pitching, and then we'll lengthen the stroke out to full swing. So let's start, if this is your golf ball and that is your target line, let's say.

BK: Okay.

CE: The first thing I want to lay down is a two-by-four, and we want to lay it on your Sweetspot Path, okay?

BK: Okay.

CE: And you want six inches from the back of the board to the ball.

BK: Okay. And what's the purpose of that?

CE: Well, because it's going to show you your angle of ascent and angle of descent. And I'll go through it here as soon as I finish this other line.

BK: Okay.

CE: That's going to establish this Sweetspot path. So this line is going to tell you where your start line is of your golf ball. So if you do this correctly, the ball should start straight over this line; if it starts to the right of it, you'll know the face match the path. If it starts to the left of it, face didn't match the path. So by having this two-by-four here, once you get

The Swing

set up, the idea is to miss it going back and to miss it coming down. If you hear the sound of the club hitting the board, you'll know that you've done something incorrectly.

BK: Okay.

CE: All right? So let's go ahead and set up how you would set up for chipping, as you set up to it, you want to try to feel the shaft a little bit steeper, so you want to set the hands up more, and you want to place the ball off of the back ankle.

BK: Okay.

CE: And the feet are about clubhead width apart, which you have right now. Now, what you want to do to steepen this angle is you need to feel like your shoulders are actually tilted this direction more. So left shoulder down, right shoulder up.

BK: Well, that just moved my club shaft back.

CE: You're going to move your hands forward.

BK: Okay.

CE: And you're going to feel like you have 75%, 80% of your weight on the left-hand side. As you move it back, all you're going to do is bend your right elbow and get your clubhead to follow that white line.

BK: Okay.

CE: So that's your Sweetspot Path.

BK: So?

CE: So as you take it back, right? Now, once you take it back there and just stop, from there, now move your hands forward through the ball, all the way over to here.

BK: Okay.

CE: So now you've controlled the face, the Sweetspot Path, the weight is left, your head -- you didn't turn, but you stayed centered the whole time, and your head stayed steady.

BK: Okay.

CE: So now, your job is to take this back, miss the board into both directions and get the ball to start straight over the top of that line.

BK: Okay.

CE: Okay.

DAVE WEDZIK: Pretty good!

CE: And now, look down here, you still have your Flat Left Wrist, you controlled the clubface. Did it go over the top of the board? I think it went right over the top of it.

DW: Pretty good, yeah.

The Swing

CE: So that means your face control and your path equaled out, so you started the ball straight. But you did that with all five keys, and here's where most people mess up. They set up because they've been told to put their head behind the golf ball. Let's go ahead and set up again, and this time let's put your head behind the ball, because we know we're supposed to do that, right? And now let's keep our angle of inclination here and start turning, take the club away, and you're going to hit the board.

BK: Hit the board every time.

CE: Okay? So if you're not set up properly, that's what's going to happen. So we want to make sure that the head is forward, spine is forward, and as you go back, if you were to hit this board coming down, that would mean that you either move backwards and you would hit the board, or you took and you didn't move the handle forward this way with your arm, you threw it from your wrist.

BK: So I was losing my Flat Left Wrist.

CE: Losing the Flat Left Wrist.

BK: Well, let me see what happens if I bend the left wrist.

CE: Ah! There you go, you're hitting both directions.

DW: So in essence, Chuck, on this little chipping motion, we're basically presetting the weight forward.

CE: Correct!

DW: We're presetting the correct shoulder tilt so that really, a Steady Head, the Weight Forward, presetting the Flat Left Wrist, those

PureStrike

things are taking care of themselves in this chipping motion.

CE: Right! And the club is not moving more than about two feet. In fact, your hands are basically moving from the middle of the right thigh to the middle of the left thigh. That's all the part of the hands you're moving. The clubhead itself of course is moving several feet farther. But that's all -- you'll learn how to hit these little shots and there should be a little divot taking when you hit this. It won't be deep, because you're not cocking the left wrist, right; you're keeping the club down. So as you go through there, you should feel a little bit of a divot.

BK: Okay, let's try this one more time.

CE: Don't move it, move it back. There you go.

DW: And Bob, one of the nice things about this drill too is you can go ahead and do this drill working on your five keys, and the fifth key, Clubface Control, you can begin -- you can start out by making sure you're chipping all the balls directly over the board. In time, you can actually practice chipping some balls to start to the right of the board, you can hit some balls to start over the board, and you can hit some balls to the left of the board, so you can actually in that chipping motion practice your Clubface --

BK: Start working.

DW: Yeah, practice your Clubface Control.

CE: So this time, without changing the Sweetspot Path, let's get the ball to start to the right of the board. What would you have to do with the clubface to do that?

BK: I would have to have the clubface open.

CE: There you go. So you can preset that

The Swing

or you can do an in swing.

BK: Very good!

CE: Okay. Good!

DW: Outstanding!

CE: Now let's get a ball start to the left. So what would the face have to do now to the path?

BK: Would have to be closed to the path.

CE: Right! So nothing changes except how you're setting this clubface, make sure you keep your head over and in the middle of your feet.

BK: Yeah, I wanted to get my head back.

CE: Yeah, you keep trying to move your head back; you want to keep your head centered, all right? All right! Long Sweetspot Path and... boom!

DW: Beautiful!

CE: And now it starts to the left.

DW: So you're understanding the beginnings of Clubface Control there too.

CE: Because imagine if this was hard to do, a swing this far, trying to control that face, how are you going to do that up here as a driver?

BK: Right!

CE: Right. So you start with

your short shots, learn how to do those, and work your way up until the full stroke.

BK: So what makes the club go back, I'm taking along the path, my right elbow is folding, so it's lifting above the board.

CE: Right! And your weight's forward.

BK: And my weight's forward.

CE: So that steepens the angle of descent.

BK: Along the path.

CE: Yeah, because if your weight was back, you'd hit the board every time.

BK: Okay, sounds good.

The Swing

The Swing: Pitching Learning the 5 Keys Using a Longer Motion

CE: You had the little chipping stroke, so now what we're going to do is we're going to do a pitch, because in chipping, remember, we don't set the club up, we don't cock the left wrist. Now, we are going to make just a shorter version of the full swing. So take your normal address position.

BK: Okay.

CE: And your normal ball position.

BK: For a --

CE: For whatever club you've got. You've got a wedge right there. So now what we want to do is we're still focusing on the five keys, so we want the club to go back along here, right? Now this ball is eight inches away from that board instead of six.

BK: Okay.

CE: So as you start back, you're going to start stretching your right side, you're going to feel the left shoulder getting closer to your left knee, with the hands coming in and your head staying steady.

BK: Okay.

CE: And the club is going right across the Sweetspot Path.

PureStrike

DW: And Chuck, that stretching of the right side that he is doing as he feels the left shoulder and that bend, that's to keep his head steady.

CE: That's to keep the head steady. So as you stretch that, right. So for a pitch length stroke, a pitch could be anywhere from here, or it could be up in here, as long as the right forearm doesn't exceed the level to the ground --

BK: Okay.

CE: -- because you're not trying to make a full swing. Now, one other thing I'd probably ask you to do is that address, instead of setting up 50-50, feel like you've got about 55% left at address.

BK: Okay.

DW: We're going to help the Weight Forward.

CE: Yeah, remember, in chipping you have 75, 80, now it's about 55.

BK: Okay.

The Swing

CE: So you take it up, you've done all that, so now what you've got to have is you've got to have your hip slide, right? Well, you keep your head steady, that brings the hands forward with the Flat Left Wrist, and you're going to exit just like you did in normal full swing.

BK: Okay.

CE: And again, you're trying to get the ball to start over this line originally.

BK: Okay.

CE: Okay. So go ahead and hit a shot and see how you do that. Okay, so --

DW: Pretty good!

CE: You hit that just a touch heavy, right? So if you hit it heavy, what would be something that you would look at, that you would think about? If I hit it heavy, what would have had to happen?

BK: Well, my weight might not have been forward.

CE: Weight might not have been forward enough and the hands might not have been forward enough.

DW: Left wrist may have bent a little bit. Left wrist may not have been flat.

BK: Okay.

DW: But there is a great point, good question there, Chuck, because that's a perfect -- that's something that may happen to, you know, any of our students. Somebody has that happen; we want to make sure that they can diagnose that. We want to make sure that you can go back and say, which one of these five keys could have caused this, or could it have

PureStrike

been two, but I need to go back, so I'm not worrying about working on too many things. If I have that problem, I want to know what to look for.

CE: Right!

BK: Okay.

CE: Okay. So let's start with, on this next swing, focus on having the handle more forward. So what would you have to do to have it more forward? You have to have more slide. More weight. More weight left.

BK: Okay. Let's see how that works.

CE: There you go!

DW: Good job!

CE: Did you feel a difference in that?

BK: Yeah, that was a lot more solid.

CE: So to you, what did you have to feel like, that you had more weight forward or --

BK: I had to feel like my weight slid forward more.

CE: Okay. And did you feel like doing that, that it got your hands farther forward as well?

BK: Yeah, it felt like as I slid my Weight Forward, my hands actually went forward, to get my Weight Forward I had to have my hands forward.

CE: Right! Right! So now we're going to add one little piece to this, this time, go ahead and address the ball.

BK: Okay.

CE: So as you come down into impact, all right, we want to start turning

The Swing

this direction and we want to keep the club out this way. In other words, don't let it come up in here and don't let your arms separate.

BK: Yeah, I'm not sure what this way means, what does --

CE: So this is your arms extending away from you.

BK: Okay.

CE: Not flipping the club up this way.

BK: So you want the club shaft still to stay in line...

CE: Yes...

BK: ...With my left arm.

CE: ...Stay in line with the left arm.

BK: Okay.

CE: And you will feel like you have to turn more to do that.

BK: Okay.

DW: You're going to maintain the feeling of that Flat Left Wrist all the way through to finish.

BK: Okay.

PureStrike

CE: So you had all the five keys on that, the ball went where you wanted it to go. You've started with a short shot, you've now moved to an intermediate shot, the next thing left is a full swing.

BK: It can't be this easy.

CE: It's that easy. In full swing, all you have to do is move just a little farther and you're done.

BK: Okay, so what are some other ways I can work on this?

CE: Well, other than having those two-by-fours we had, you can just take an old shaft or a rod, you know, something like that, lay it on the ground, and use it as your golf ball. So go ahead and set your club right over here on this side of it.

BK: Okay.

CE: And as you come down, you want to make sure that you're missing that line and striking the ground in front of it.

The Swing

BK: So I don't want to --

CE: No.

BK: I want to get it in front of the --

CE: You've got to get it in front. So to do that, you've got to have a lot of Weight Forward and you've got to have the hands forward.

DW: Nice! This would be learning to take a divot in front of the golf ball, controlling the low point.

CE: There you go!

DW: Very nice! And you could use quite anything here; you could scrape a line in the dirt, you could go into your bunker, you could draw a line in the bunker, you could do it in the sand.

CE: And start off with small swings like you're doing right now and then just start increasing the length of the swing.

BK: And just, should I put balls down and hit balls in there?

CE: Well, you're trying to hit on the other side of this line. If you put a ball there, you'll probably --

BK: So if I just set up myself.

CE: There you go!

BK: Just make sure I'm -- that makes me definitely feel like I'm moving.

CE: You've got to get left in order to hit on this side of that line.

DW: And I should say that this is a drill -- the main priority in this drill is working on the Weight Forward and the Flat Left Wrist.

BK: Sounds good!

The Swing

The Swing: Full Swing Learning the 5 Keys Using a Full Swing Motion

DW: You've done a great job with the chipping and the pitching, now we're going to talk about how we go -- how simple it is to go from pitching to the full swing.

CE: So go ahead and set the ball.

BK: Okay.

CE: And let's make your pitch back length swing. All right! So from there, all you're going to do is turn your shoulders more and let your arms go with it, and you're done. Your hands have moved about 6 inches and that's the end of it.

BK: That's the end of my swing.

CE: Then you go the other way.

BK: Hmm.

CE: So all you've got to do is just complete your backswing with your arms up a little more and you're done. So it's the very same motion as the pitch; you just have a little more shoulder turn.

BK: So really from pitch to the full swing, I'm just stretching that right side --

CE: A little more.

BK: -- a little bit more.

CE: Yeah. And completing your shoulder turn.

DW: To keep that head steady.

BK: All right! Let's try this.

DW: Beautiful!

The Swing

CE: And that's about as simple as it gets.

DW: Talk about easy.

CE: So did you feel like -- how much extra did you feel like you had to move?

BK: Nothing.

CE: Right! Because like I said, you're only moving that far from the pitch.

BK: Well, what's really nice is I'm learning the path to go back from the chip to the pitch and all, it is a little bit of a completion to the full swing.

CE: Right, because in the chip you had a very small back motion, the club was traveling along the Sweetspot Path; with the pitch, you had a little bit more shoulder turn, a little bit of the stretching on the right side with the Steady Head. In the full swing, you stretched that right side fully with more shoulder turn, Steady Head, and then you just swing down through the ball.

BK: Well, that seemed pretty simple. You know, really, all for me it was is, once I understood and I get an idea of the keys, it was from the short chipping stroke to the pitching stroke, it's really following the same path, just a little bit longer, and then from the pitching to the full swing, you know, as long as I have in my mind what has to happen in those five keys, it's pretty simple.

CE: Right! And they apply to every stroke you hit, so they just -- maybe at a different time, but they all apply. So again, when you start your shoulder stroke and you work your way up, all you're doing is just expanding those keys the length of the stroke, that's all you're doing, but the keys never change.

DW: Can't get any easier than that!

BK: That's easy!

PureStrike

Swing Speed: Maximizing Speed with the 5 Keys

DAVE WEDZIK: So I'm here today with James Hirshfield, one of our Medicus instructors. And James, I know we get a lot of questions from our students talking about how they can start to hit the ball further, how they're going to go about building more speed in their game, and really, you know, what I'd like to term as dynamic speed.

JAMES HIRSHFIELD: Absolutely!

DW: And I think one of the first things they need to realize is, it's important that they master or can perform the majority or all of the five keys to be able to hit the ball solidly, accurately do that, before they really move on to trying to hit the ball, you know, a country mile so to speak.

JH: Most definitely, it would be -- it's very difficult to try and swing the club as fast as you can when you can't even make solid contact if your head is moving around over the place. So definitely mastering the five keys would be the first place to start and then being able to start swinging faster is going to be a massive advantage as well.

DW: Right! So let's say you've got a good handle on the five keys and you really do want to start building this sort of dynamic speed, right? You want to start hitting that ball further and further, because let's face it, it makes it easier to play golf courses hitting wedges into greens than it does hitting five irons into greens.

JH: Yeah.

DW: You know, lot of times I think we see this in baseball, golf, and other places where people come out and they'll grab either a bat or a golf club, and it's almost like they're trying to swing almost with more of an accuracy in mind, or they're just trying to do it at a certain motion speed, and sometimes it helps just to quite literally say, hey, let's speed up the arms. Let's swing those things faster. Let's do that.

Swing Speed

JH: And that is one part of it, but it's very difficult to start hitting a golf ball far if you're just using your arms to try and swing this club. You've got to start understanding how you have to use your body, to be able to use your body in the ground to project this golf ball as far as you can.

DW: Right, so you can swing your arms pretty fast there.

JH: To an extent, but limited, yeah.

DW: To an extent. But as we start building up power from the other places and using our body along with our arms, the pivot, these other things, we can really start to hit the ball.

JH: Absolutely! Absolutely!

DW: So let's go over a couple of things here. If I have you take your setup and I'll have you kind of demonstrate some of this and, you know, we'll go through it, but first thing would be, I think we see in talking about some of the other keys, I think we can go right to a Steady Head and kind of explain, you know, some of the things about that. I think a lot of people are under the misnomer that in making a golf swing they should be staying in their spine angle. Okay? And I think what's important to point out is, if James makes a backswing, and I'll tell you another one too, staying in your spine angle, turning around a flexed right knee, doing some of those things, right?

JH: That's making it harder from the beginning.

DW: I'd like to have James, James, have you demonstrate a backswing here where you would actually sort of try to maintain your spine angle or stay kind of bend over, and maintain the flex in the forward leg and so everyone can kind of see what that does to sort of some of the power pieces.

JH: So this is the golfer who is being told they need to keep their right leg flexed and try and coil into that right leg.

DW: Absolutely!

PureStrike

JH: What starts to happen is their head moves. So first of all, the Steady Head piece is gone out the window.

DW: Yeah, we've lost key number one.

JH: And as you start to see by keeping my right knee as bent as I can, my hips aren't turning, my shoulders can't turn, and you start to see, one, my head is moving around. And I can't turn, I'm pretty flexible and I can't turn my shoulders more than, what, maybe 70, 60, 70 degrees.

DW: Yeah, you can see here quite clear this is at most 60 or 70 degrees shoulder turn, with a very limited hip turn. Okay. So if we really wanted to hit the ball the furthest, I would say, quite simply, we'd want to maximize some...

JH: Absolutely!

DW: ...Of the turning components. Maximize the hip turn, maximize kind of the shoulder turn. So let's talk a little bit about how we'd go about doing that.

JH: So you need to be able to turn your shoulders 90 degrees, and one of the ways that you do that is actually

68

Swing Speed

by letting your hips turn as well. So you have to understand that the right leg, some of the longest hitters, Bubba Watson, Dustin Johnson, Phil Mickelson, you've seen these golfers --

DW: John Daly.

JH: Absolutely, all the longest hitters, they start straightening their right leg at the same time as they keep doing the stretching piece of the right hip and the right side.

DW: Right, right! Now, that's a lot -- that's a backswing. That's a turn there. Now, that's allowing, by straightening this right leg, you've allowed this whole side to stretch, right? You've maximized the hip turn, which has allowed the shoulders now to turn past 90 degrees.

JH: You can see how much further the left arm has traveled; it's gone much, much further. So now I have the ability to store more power in a golf swing as well.

DW: Right! So when it comes time to swing those arms really fast, we've got more stored energy to start to whip down that golf ball.

JH: Absolutely! Absolutely!

DW: Okay. So we reach the top with sort of, again, what we'll call, you know, maximizing those components to turn the furthest there, and now we've got to start figuring out, now, like we talked about, how that's -- we're going to really speed up those arms and how to transfer some of that stored energy out into those arms by the time impact comes. Okay. So if you go ahead and take the club up to the top, right, I want to talk a little bit about how from there, and this would be going into, you know, a little bit more of the five keys. James is going to want to make sure he starts to shift his Weight Forward, okay, while his arms, basically, this angle here is really not changing early in the downswing, okay? So he is not throwing the club head down at the golf ball. He's not trying to speed up his arms there, he's storing the energy as he starts his hips forward, and I call it, you know, we're going to see a big chain reaction start to go off here pretty quick, right?

JH: Absolutely! Most definitely! A lot of golfers are going to the top of the swing and their instinct is to try and get that clubhead to the ball as fast as they can.

DW: Right!

JH: What they start to do is just throw their hands away, start throwing the arms down as fast as they can, and now they don't start using the body and the ground to create any power.

DW: Right!

JH: So there has to be a sequencing there.

DW: And that brings us to a great point what you just said there about using the ground for power, or lever, that's a big thing we talk about a lot. And so as you start moving forward here, you can really notice here, if we look at the way James' knees are working with his Weight Forward, right, he's starting to press down into the ground, and the key here is that he is going to really start to use the leverage of the ground there, to not only

Swing Speed

be able to keep rotating and turning, but also he's going to press that ground, right, to almost feel like you're going to spring up, or use it for leverage, you're going to...

JH: ...Absolutely!

DW: ...Pounce off that ground.

JH: Definitely!

DW: We love to use the example when you start talking about how you're going to use the ground for leverage and for power, I can think of a few different examples. One would be the discus thrower. You can, you know, if you look at a picture of a discuss thrower, they're wound up and fully coiled, the legs compressed down into the ground, and then they are just pushing off that ground, and not only are pushing off the ground and turning and everything is stored and fine. Yeah. One of my other favorite ones would be a slapshot in hockey.

JH: Okay.

DW: A hockey player, which is, you know, similar to a golf -- the hockey stick is similar to a golf club in a lot of ways, right? It's a bent implement.

JH: Yeah.

PureStrike

DW: So -- when a hockey player is going -- getting ready hit to a slapshot, they are not able to hit that slapshot with their skates sliding around on the ice. In fact, if you tried to hit a hard slapshot in bare feet, it would be impossible, you'd never get any power on it. The first thing the hockey player does is dig the skates into the ice so they can use that ice for lots of leverage to be able to transfer that energy out into the puck.

JH: Yeah.

DW: Okay? So we've gotten ourselves sort of, you know, halfway down here and now we're really ready to unleash all this, okay? And now we're going to start -- this is when the arms, right, you can really start to feel, these arms are really starting to fly at that point.

JH: So from here I've started creating the best chain reaction, the lower body started to go forward, and to go into a little bit of detail about the best players, not only are they sliding their hips forward, but also doing it very quickly.

DW: Right!

JH: Not just in one go, but they're doing it very quickly, into the downswing.

DW: Right!

JH: So they start creating really nice chain reaction there. So if we could see this on like a 3D graph or something, from like TPI or something like that, we'd see really fast motions and lot of spikes in that graph at this point.

JH: It would start off very low and go very high and it would be very quick as well, very steep.

DW: Right! Right! So as we start coming down, you're feeling all that stored energy happening, everything is flying right out into those arms, and it's at this point really that everything kind of lets loose. Your hips have moved forward, your weight is forward. Right now your body starts

Swing Speed

rotating, you're really storing up that energy, and you just start exploding off the ground, right, you're using your legs --

JH: Yeah, absolutely!

DW: -- pushing like crazy and exploding up into full extension, I'd say, right, just stretching, stretching like crazy into that follow-through.

JH: Most definitely! At the very end of my swing I want to feel like I'm stretched as much as I can, again, from all the way up my legs, up my torso, my arms, everything should feel stretched out as much as possible.

DW: Kind of like Jason Zuback would do that or something.

JH: Yeah, absolutely!

DW: The most possible power, right, stretching.

JH: Absolutely!

PureStrike

DW: Just stretching like crazy in that follow-through.

JH: You'd see that the shortest hitters, their follow-through would look like this.

DW: Yeah.

JH: They need to keep stretching all the way through to make that club, come like that.

DW: Yeah, that's when golfers would struggle with the distance the most, right?

JH: Absolutely! When they would have no stretching or no extension on the backswing and then no stretching or no extension on the follow-

Swing Speed

through. Okay. So I guess we've kind of put that altogether. Seems there's a lot to it, but at the same time really in the end it turns out to be, you know, something where you're basically going to keep just stretching on that backswing, right, just keep stretching out.

JH: So I would say put it into like a kind of nice little phrase whilst I'm practicing, I'd be thinking, stretch, slide, and stretch again to the follow-through.

DW: Perfect! Perfect! Why don't you go ahead and rip one out there, let's see you smash one? Beautiful! Great job! Great job!

Educated Hands: The Secret to Clubface Control

DAVE WEDZIK: Is this where you talk about educating the hands a little bit?

CHUCK EVANS: Right, educating the hands is a whole key. I mean, the hands are what's holding the club. The club is not attached to our chest, it's not attached to our legs or hips, it's attached to the hands. That's how we hold the club. So we've got to know what we're doing with these hands at any given moment. We have to give them a job, give them an assignment, they complete their assignment, and if they do that correctly, and they're educated, then the ball does what it's supposed to do. Those hands are going to control what the face is doing; they're also going to control where they're going in the swing. To give you an example, Bob, if you just setup. Can you see my -- All right! Can you see my hand right here?

BOB KOCH: Yes.

CE: All right! Take your hands to my hand. You notice he had a nice turn

Educated Hands

in the backswing. Take your hands to my hand. You'll notice that now he is on his left side, with his head centered, and he is at impact, and now take your hands to my hand. And now he is all the way through the shot. So did you once think about what your body was doing?

BK: No, I just took my hands to where you were telling me to take them.

CE: All right! Because his hands are educated. So if you tell your hands what to do and they do their job, then everything else should work. So you'll sometimes see on the PGA Tour, if you're watching TV, player will hit a shot and they'll seem like they're way out of balance, and the announcer says, "Boy, because he's got a great pair of hands he saved the shot." Well, most people that play golf unfortunately don't have great hands. They have to learn that education. They have to train their hands what to do. So your body can be in a lot of different places, but if you have educated hands, it can make up for some mistakes. Conversely, if you have good body motion, but you can't control the clubface, because your hands are uneducated, you still can't hit the ball to target. So those are things that we encapsulate those five keys to.

DW: Would you say those five simple keys, if we do those correctly, they make a PureStrike much easier, they make the hands' job much easier?

CE: Oh, much, much simpler, much simpler. And again, for an illustration, I mean, if you reach for a glass of water, you wouldn't move your body and then extend your arm, right, you just extend your arm. So we do this every single day. I mean, if you didn't have educated hands and you were eating, you'd never hit your mouth. You just stick yourself --

DW: I've done that too every single day.

CE: Okay. So those are educated hands. Now, the same education we used to doing all those other things, we apply to this golf club.

Purestrike

The Grip

CE: You know, obviously for beginning golfers, they need to know two things. First, how do you hold this thing, all right, and secondly, what's a good posture to get into? So let's talk about the grip.

DW: So we've got to get it in the hands somewhat there.

CE: Yeah. So let's talk about the location and the angle of the hand relative to the grip.

DW: Okay. Perfect! So if I open my hand up here, we get a shot of this, what we're going to be able to see is how when I put this club into my hand, I want to make sure that it rests more down in these finger joints here, and at maximum it's not going to get up past the low part of this heel pad right here. So somewhere right down on those finger joints, at the very base of that heel pad, down in the low part of that heel pad. Where we're going to go wrong is if we start to slide this club up into the lifeline there of the hand and start to get this club too much in the palm like that, we want it to rest much more down on the fingers, all right, keep the correct pressure points on that grip and then just wrap the hand over there. Now, what about like the location of my hand, like we hear about strong or weak or --

CE: Yeah, I mean, you know, there are players that play with this type of grip that hit fades;

Educated Hands

there are players that take this kind of grip that hit draws. So there is really no constant as far as this, but the angle relative to the hand is the most significant part. I think as a player you have to figure out which angle now you want to put it on that gives you the best sensation for the Clubface Control.

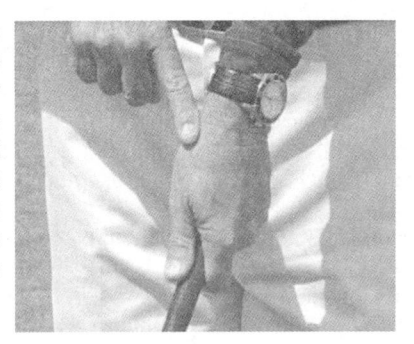

DW: So I understand the Clubface Control.

CE: And that's through experimentation.

DW: Right, because grip and this left wrist, that's going to really be a big part to understanding Clubface Control. So what you're sort of saying there in one way would be that this grip is somewhat a variable, even amongst really good players.

CE: Right!

DW: Good players play with a very -- a grip that might look like that, or a grip that might look like that, and they still can play pretty well.

CE: Right! Right! So now we've got the left hand on, so now, how will we put the right hand on it?

DW: I'm just going to -- you know, I mean, I use an overlapping grip. I'm going to keep that thing down on my fingers as well here, and I use an overlapping grip and I'm just going to kind of wrap that on top, but really whether you use an overlapping grip or an interlocking grip or a ten finger grip, I'm just going to kind of take that right hand keep it in the fingers and match it over that left hand, about like so.

CE: So your right hand grip would look where this pad is covering this thumb this way.

DW: Yeah, absolutely! Right in the crux of that crease. Yeah, so you want to take that lifeline, that pad, and just put it right there over that thumb.

CE: Yeah. And then we want to place the right thumb where?

DW: Just, just on the forward side of the shaft there, just slightly, we're not going to put that right going back in there too much on top of the grip, just on the forward side.

CE: Right! And let me ask you one more question. You see a lot of people sometimes will have this hand way under the club --

DW: -- Yeah.

CE: -- and then some people have it, you know, way over the top, to Harley-Davidson grip, and one thing that we're pretty adamant about as far as just right hand grip, we talked about in Clubface Control and in Sweetspot Control about this right forefinger and how it monitors that Sweetspot. Well, the only way you can do that is if it's on this back or aft side of the club shaft, because if it gets under it or over it, you no longer can sense and direct a Sweetspot. So this hand is much more critical than this hand is.

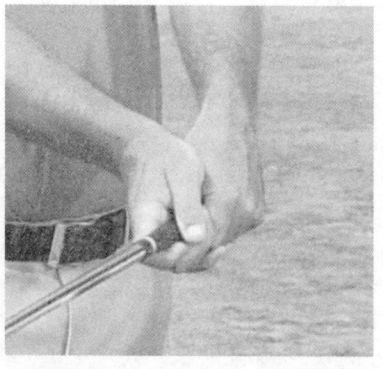

DW: It's going to be on the side so it can control that Sweetspot pressure.

CE: Right, right! So just a little quick thing, if you were going to move your hands forward, where do you feel the pressure right now?

Educated Hands

DW: Start to feel pressure in that finger.

CE: Start to feel the pressure in that finger.

DW: Right, in that joint, right there that we talked about, right there that controls the Sweetspot.

CE: And if I wanted the handle to lean forward, would I apply pressure to the back of the shaft or to the front of the shaft?

DW: You'll apply pressure on the backside.

CE: All right, so the pressure on the backside of the shaft is that forefinger.

DW: Yeah.

CE: These last three fingers, and the pressure from this pad pushing against that thumb.

DW: Right under there.

CE: Right.

DW: I can really -- you really feel that when you do that, when you move that handle forward, I can really feel that quite nicely.

CE: Right! And that's what you want to feel. So that's the basic grip part. Now we're going to talk about how you want to set up to a shot for any normal full swing shot, not necessarily a short game, but a full swing.

Posture

CE: Yeah, and you can kind of point out a couple of things as we're doing this, but -- so for me, I like to just right off the bat try to get relaxed, and we're not going to be trying to take a lot of the tension out, we're going to kind of relax here. And one of the ways I like to talk to people about it is, I'd start by just standing like the two of us are standing here talking, right?

CE: Right!

DW: We're standing here, I grab my golf club, and really, all you need to do is just kind of add a little bit of knee flex, okay?

CE: Right!

DW: And we're going to simply bend over from the waist. What I'm really, honestly, trying to avoid is adding any tension by trying to really straighten my back, trying to arch things there.

CE: Or push these hips like way up in the air.

DW: Right! Push this out like this and straighten my back like this, right, that kind of hurts.

CE: Right!

DW: Really, honestly. So yeah, flexed knees, just a little bit of knee flex. I'm just kind of, kind of bend over to the ground, I'm going to let my hips flex, and really I'm going to feel like my shoulders round, okay?

CE: Yeah. And you're going to be pretty balanced. So if I was to push you, you wouldn't be moving too much.

DW: No, not at all, not at all.

CE: And then the other key is the shoulder area and the shoulder girdle up here needs to feel like it's a little bit rounded, because you don't want it straight back -- the shoulders back in this direction.

DW: Right, exactly!

Educated Hands

CE: Because now that's going to add tension and your arms are not going to swing. So we've got this rounded. Now let's talk about, how about your eyes?

DW: You know, we see, and I talk to so many students who have trouble, they're playing with bifocals, or they're playing with sunglasses, they can't see the ball quite properly, and they're under the impression that they've got to have a little bit kind of a straight back and they've got to have their chin up somehow so they can like turn their shoulder underneath there. So the important thing would be -- and that's why, again, when you get the sunglasses, things like that, you've got your chin up so much, it does get hard to see that golf ball. So what we really want to do is just take and rotate the neck down, we want to feel like we're seeing the ball straight down out of this central vision of our eyes. We're just looking straight down at it.

CE: So let me ask you, Dave, have you ever been to World Golf Village and seen the Hall of Fame there?

DW: Yeah, I've been there, yeah, a couple of times.

CE: Well, you know, when they put the Hogan thing in there, for Ben Hogan, it shows his locker, you know, that he had at Shady Oaks with all these salves and balms that he had to put on, bandages, but it also had his clothes in there. If you looked at his shirts and sweaters, every single one of them had a wear spot at the left shoulder, because Hogan's key was, you know, he used to over swing, just like John Daly, was when his left shoulder hit his chin, that's when he stopped his backswing. So when your head is down here like this, it's fairly easy for your chin to hit your shoulder.

DW: Absolutely!

CE: But if you've got your neck up here like this, trying to look down through your eyes, you never would do it. So a good key for some of you that are over-swinging might be just to keep your head down this way a little farther, and when your shoulder hits your chin, stop the backswing, right?

DW: Easy!

CE: So we want a nice and relaxed posture. We want the club more in the fingers, and the right hand, we want to make sure that we've got that index finger on the backside of the shaft so we can apply pressure from the backside forward. So now you've got your -- now you've got your basic grip, you've got your basic setup.

DW: This feels very relaxed and very comfortable.

CE: I mean, it should feel relaxed.

DW: Shoulders are rounded, neck matches.

CE: Yeah, and you don't want that tight feeling. How are you going to move the club, right?

DW: I feel soft and relaxed and on balance.

CE: Yeah, good! All right! So there you have it, grip and setup.

Drills

PureStrike: Drills for the 5 Keys

Steady Head Drills

CHUCK EVANS: All right! So let's go ahead and show them some of the drills they can use for some of the keys and let's start with the Steady Head and let's give them like a couple of drills for each key that they can do at home very simply.

DAVE WEDZIK: Sounds great! The easy one; you want to maybe do the wall drill.

CE: Yeah, let's start with that.

DW: ...Against the wall. Okay. So I'm going to go ahead and take my setup, and if you're doing this at home or student -- anybody who is watching this doing this at home, you're basically going to take your head and you're going to rest it right up against the wall on a stationary spot on the wall. So if you put your hand there.

CE: So with my hand there, that's going to represent the wall. Now, you won't have a golf club doing this, however, because you won't be able to get your head into the wall. You'll just be holding your hands this way.

DW: Right, exactly! So I'm going to go ahead and make a swing, and my focus is going to simply be on stretching this side, okay, my left shoulder is going to be going down a little bit as I do it, and that's all going to keep my head stable in its place. Just about like that, okay? Now, as we're doing this, if we start to diagnose in doing this drill, if I'm doing this drill and I feel my head start to slide along the wall to the right, okay, I'm going to start to -- I'm going to have to understand that I need to bend more to the left or stretch more, and make sure that I feel that stretch to hold my head in place, okay? If I start to do this drill and I see where my head's actually going forward or sliding on the wall to the left way, I'm going to make sure that I'm still turning my shoulders enough and not just stretching. If I just stretch, my head can actually go forward. I want to make sure that I turn my shoulders as I stretch and that's going to keep the head perfectly stable.

CE: Right! And what about if the head goes up?

DW: So if the head -- we'll talk about that, right? So if the head -- now, I'm doing this drill, we do the backswing and I start to notice my head's rising.

CE: And leaving the wall.

DW: Leaving the wall, okay, that's when I want to make sure I feel enough of this bending, right, or my left shoulder going downward enough during the backstroke, okay, to keep it stable.

CE: Right! Now, let's talk about it from the backstroke down.

DW: Well, let's actually real quick here, let's even talk about if the head goes down.

CE: Okay.

DW: Let's talk about that. So if my head -- if I see where I'm doing this and I start noticing my head is going down like this, that goes back to a little bit of the stretching, but also enough of the extending this way. So I'm going to go ahead that I make sure that I feel more of the stretching

Drills

and sort of straightening from the hips or the extending to keep my head in place.

CE: Right! Right!

DW: So that's an easy way to diagnose that.

CE: So that's an easy way to diagnose that. So that's in the backswing, so now let's talk about -- basically it's the same thing, we're trying to keep the head steady in the downswing.

DW: Exactly! So from the top I want to go ahead and practice my downswing, where I just simply slide my hips forward, keeping my head right in its place, allowing me to create axis tilt while keeping my head in its spot. And the key there is that I slide my hips forward to do that and create the axis tilt. That's what's going to keep my head stable. If I start noticing that when I do this that my head is going backward this way, that would very likely be me starting to create this axis tilt manually or putting it on my own, and I just want to make sure that I keep my head stable and steady by pushing my hips forward, keep my head right in its place.

CE: Right! So the axis tilt that we discussed, there's actually two of those, right?

DW: Yeah, yeah. There's one forward at address and then there is one where your spine is leaning this direction, and as you slide the hips, it is now going the opposite direction.

DW: It changes direction.

PureStrike

CE: So it's the upper changing direction.

DW: Yeah, it's that upper half changing directions. So when I push those hips forward, push the hips forward, this tilt right here, this tilt on my side.

CE: Yeah, that creates that tilt.

DW: Yeah.

CE: So now let's say that your head is going too far to the right or too far to the left, so now we can move from the wall to a doorjamb.

DW: Yeah, let's say a doorjamb. So let's say, you're saying, let's say you know you have this problem, your head has been moving too far, let's say your head has been moving too far back during the backstroke, okay, what we might do then is I might go ahead and set up inside a door.

CE: Okay. This would be the doorjamb.

DW: And I'll go ahead and put that doorjamb right to the side of my head there on the right so that when I make these swings, my head has no way to move to the right. Pretty simple there. The nice thing about that drill is that if you know that's your problem, it's pretty hard to mess that one up. So that's a really simple drill. Put that doorjamb there, you make sure that doesn't happen.

CE: Right!

Drills

DW: We do see sometimes with people, maybe you've got a student, they're watching, you know, their video and their head is moving forward.

CE: Right!

DW: Okay. So you can do it just the opposite basically.

CE: So we put the doorjamb on this side.

DW: We set up the doorjamb over here, right, and you're going to make sure you do the backswing where your head doesn't move forward. And again, with that doorjamb there, it's really impossible for it to move forward.

CE: Right! So just those two drills alone will focus on keeping the Steady Head.

DW: Absolutely! It keeps it real simple, it makes it real, real easy to do the Steady Head properly.

CE: And you can do this at home.

DW: Yeah!

CE: Without a net.

Weight Forward Drills

CE: Okay. So for the next key we want to talk about Weight Forward.

DW: Right!

CE: All right? So let's do a couple of those drills and, again, we can go right back to the doorjamb.

DW: Yeah, we really can, because we were starting to talk about that, right, and you can kind of tie in the Weight Forward with the Steady

Head.

CE: Right!

DW: It's real nice.

CE: So if you set up with the doorjamb over here on the left side of your head.

DW: Okay. If all he did now was push his Weight Forward, that's how you practice Weight Forward.

DW: Okay. And I can do that even without a club.

CE: You can do it without a club as well.

DW: Right here from an address position we're going to isolate the hips forward, which is going to put the Weight Forward, and we're just, again, with a doorjamb or without it, I'm going to keep my head still, and push my hips forward. That's putting all the weight onto this forward leg. Okay. That's just training the sensation of what it feels like to have my Weight Forward. It's isolating that condition.

CE: And as you're pushing that forward, that is tilting your spine to the back.

DW: Yeah, absolutely, you can start to see that tilt. All right! So if you were to actually -- if you were to hold that club --

CE: If you had that vertically.

DW: Right, you can see everything is vertical right there and when I push my hips forward and put the Weight Forward.

Drills

CE: Now it's more this way.

DW: I'm going to see how that creates this tilt, okay?

CE: So that's two simple ways to work on your Weight Forward and keeping your head steady.

DW: Yeah, yeah.

CE: But right now you can take an old shaft or you can take one of those driveway markers.

DW: Yeah. Perfect! Something easy to find.

CE: Yeah, and you can do this, you know, at the range in your backyard, as you get set you want to put this out just outside the left hip.

DW: Just an inch or two, a couple of inches outside the foot, just outside the knee and the hip.

CE: And what you may find in the downswing is you may find that your knee actually gets there before the hip does.

DW: Yeah, because that flex knee allows me to keep moving the hips, my Weight Forward.

CE: Yeah. So show them what that would look like without hitting a ball first.

DW: Yeah, yeah. And the nice thing is too, like you mentioned, you know, the same premise behind this drill, you can do this at home if you have a chair on wheels or anything, you're just basically trying to set it up in front of you and push it out of the way, to feel that weight transfer forward. So if I was to do this I'm going to make a nice backswing with a Steady Head, then I'm going to feel my left leg, it's maintaining its flex, my hips are pushing forward, my weight's all forward, I'm starting to push that stick out of the way. You can actually see that stick move, it will keep moving.

CE: The stick will be moving. So go ahead and hit a shot.

DW: I'll go ahead and hit one. I want to make a good backswing with a Steady Head, pushing my left knee and hips forward, push that stick right out of the way.

CE: All right! Excellent!

DW: Really solid there!

CE: Excellent!

DW: I can feel myself actually hit that as I make that swing, transfer that Weight Forward.

CE: Yeah. I mean, and when the people see this, they're going to see that this thing has pushed this direction.

DW: Yeah.

CE: So that tells them that the weight is moving forward.

DW: Right!

CE: Now, we've got a lot of wind today, but it's not enough to move the ball. So good job!

Flat Left Wrist Drills

CE: All right! So let's talk -- let's give them a couple of drills now on the Flat Left Wrist. And again, these are things that they can do at home. So this is one you can do actually in a doorjamb. So we'll say my foot is a doorjamb.

Drills

DW: All right! So I'm going to basically go ahead and use your foot to represent the doorjamb, okay? I'm going to take my -- I can do this a couple ways; I can do it rehearsing a small backswing into this, or I can do it just actually rehearsing the Flat Left Wrist field impact. I'll start by just kind of explaining and sort of rehearsing the Flat Left Wrist field impact. So I'm going to go ahead, and as I do this, I'm setting this right behind with really no pressure into your foot or the doorjamb, I want to push my Weight Forward and start to feel this left wrist get flat, and I'm actually also feeling a little bit of upward movement in the shaft. So I'm feeling downward pressure going down into the ground or into the doorjamb and I'm feeling that left wrist very flat. So I can feel a lot of pressure there against your foot.

CE: And you've got a lot of pressure right here on that forefinger.

DW: A lot of pressure in that same forefinger or that pointer right there.

CE: And your wrist, actually what your left wrist is doing is actually going a little bit down. It's uncocking, which is moving the clubhead downward for that pressure.

DW: Right, that's where I'm feeling all that pressure.

CE: Yeah, because if you didn't have it uncocked --

PureStrike

DW: It's no longer there.

CE: -- you no longer have pressure in the ground.

DW: Nothing. Yeah.

CE: So that's the motion happening is that left wrist is uncocking downward while the shaft's bending forward, and you can see some straightening of the shaft right there.

DW: Yeah, I can feel that thing like it's going to bend, yeah. And it's really interesting, because the difference between this uncocked as opposed to the difference between it being hinged or cocked here and then being uncocked, lots of pressure here, and it actually feels like the handle is just raised up a little bit as I'm doing that. Yeah, that's good!

CE: So the shaft angle has changed, it moved upward slightly.

DW: Yeah. Yeah. Now, I could do that also, I can do this -- again, I'm going to just trace a backswing. Do a small backswing, keep my Weight Forward; Weight Forward, Weight Forward, present impact there, and again, feel that Flat Left Wrist, lots of pressure, I can feel it right here against that forefinger.

CE: Right!

DW: And that handle feels like it's just kind of raised a little bit there, with the wrist uncocked.

CE: Now, just for giggles here, let's go back to address, and make your mini backswing, but as you come down, instead of moving your Weight Forward, start turning and see if you can still put that club in the center of my foot.

DW: Sounds good! So if you start turning early.

DW: I'm going on turning --

Drills

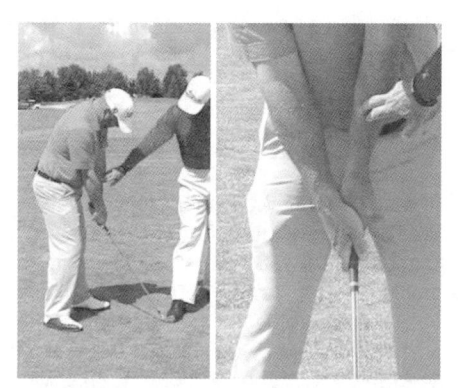

CE: Now the hands are coming early and they're wanting to move --

DW: Yeah, you can see.

CE: -- even left.

DW: Yeah. They're actually going to keep trying to go this direction.

CE: Yeah. So you'd hit the inside part of the doorjamb.

DW: Yeah, absolutely, absolutely! Almost like toeing the doorjamb.

CE: Right, right!

DW: Yeah. I can feel my left wrist flexing.

CE: Toejamb!

DW: All right! So let's talk a little more about that whole Flat Left Wrist and that key and maybe another drill that we can work on to fix that up.

CE: Right! I mean, you know, a lot of times you see people, you know, they're drawing lines on the ground hitting balls, or trying to get the club to enter the ground. And we did one, you and I did one earlier, you know, in another segment where we were actually hitting balls in front of a white line, right?

DW: Right, right!

CE: Well, you could just -- you can do this, you know, if your kids have a sandbox or you're at the golf club, what you want to do is go to the bunker and build yourself a little wall, a little wall of sand. And the idea for it is you place this wall where you would normally have your ball position for whatever club you're going to use. When you're coming into impact, you want to destroy the whole wall, you don't want to clip the top of the wall. That would mean that the clubhead is going this way. So if I have my weight back and the clubhead forward, I might not even hit the wall. I might go clear over the top of it.

DW: And you've made this wall pretty tall. It looks like you've built up a good 3, 4 inches of sand here.

CE: Right!

DW: And yeah, like you're saying, we don't want to take out the top half of the wall.

CE: Right!

DW: We want to take out the whole wall.

CE: We want to take the whole wall out from ground level.

DW: Okay.

CE: Right! And the sensation that you're going to feel when you do this, it's almost going to feel the sensation of the club stopping, and the impact is going to feel so heavy, it's unbelievable.

Drills

DW: Lots of pressure.

CE: Lots of pressure, lots of down, lots of heavy, because this is not heavy impact, and destroying this wall will give you heavy impact. So let me set up and hit one.

DW: Okay.

CE: And I'll do one little flip first.

DW: Yeah, okay, sounds good.

CE: So this is the person that -- you know, we're going to set the club here, this is the person that kind of hangs back on their right leg and then flips the club past their hands.

DW: So maybe bends that left wrist.

CE: Yeah, left wrist bends, clubhead goes past the hands.

DW: Weight's certainly not forward, I'm missing that key.

CE: Right! Weight's on the back foot. So now you can see that all I do is just clip the very top, right? And there wasn't even a sensation of impact, you know? So now what I want to do is I want to make sure as I come down I move the Weight Forward, and the handle, the grip forward so that I bring, not only the clubhead to this wall, I want to imagine the whole shaft coming into that wall.

DW: Hitting that wall.

97

PureStrike

CE: But coming in at a forward angle, I don't want to come in at a vertical angle of the shaft, right?

DW: Perfect! Perfect!

CE: So I get set, take it back. And I'm in, that baby makes it completely different.

DW: There is some weight in that, there is some pressure, and that's heavy.

CE: And you can -- oh, and you can feel the club stop.

DW: Yeah, little harder to swing through it.

CE: It is.

DW: Really heavy.

CE: But that's the same feel you've got to have when you're hitting a normal golf shot.

DW: Yeah, absolutely!

CE: You're hitting down on the ball and the handle forward. So step into it, go ahead and give it a twirl.

DW: Yeah, let me see that. So I'm going to make sure my weight is forward. I want to feel that heavy hit with lots of pressure down at the bottom.

CE: Oh yeah.

DW: Man! Man!

Drills

CE: Big, big difference in the sound between those two and that first one where the clubhead went past, right?

DW: That feels good! Easy to work on too.

CE: Oh! You know, just don't do it when you're facing in -- when the wind's blowing into you, so you need to button up.

DW: I feel the shot.

CE: Yeah. So this is a great drill to do at your club, or even in your kids' sandbox. Get that heavy field of impact, that's going to get the shaft forward, Weight Forward, and you're going to wind up what we call compressing the golf ball a lot better.

DW: Really nice!

Sweet Spot Path Drills

CE: All right! So now let's do a couple of drills on Sweetspot, on how to get that Sweetspot Path to match up, and you see all I've got here is just an ordinary golf shaft and I've got one of those driveway markers stuck in the end of it.

DW: Yeah.

CE: So I'm going to hand it to you and let you set it up and you can explain that.

DW: This is great for that, yeah. So I'm going to go ahead and I'm going to set up to where, you know, I would be going to hit my golf ball. And the nice thing about this drill is too, we can not only do this for practice at home or, you know, on the range, wherever, but you can hit some golf balls like this too, so this is a really good drill for that. So first thing I'm going to do is I'm going to get this set up correctly, that would be the most important thing. So once I've taken my set up, the easiest way to do this, I'm going to rest this basically on my shoulder, so it's, you know, pretty much touching my shoulder. Then I'm going to simply take it back, about six inches or so, and push it into the ground, so it's on about the same angle as it was when it was resting on my shoulder. Okay? Pretty simple. I'm going to go ahead and take my setup, and the point of this is really to -- little bit more here for the backswing path, and we're going to talk about how the -- not only how the Sweetspot travels on its path and the hands travel on their path to make that a little bit simpler.

CE: Right!

DW: Okay? So again, with that in the ground I'm going to go ahead and I'm going to make my backswing, and I'll start out by, let's say, my Sweetspot Path goes outside a little bit, my arms go up a little bit. My left arm's going to run into this pretty quickly.

CE: Right! So that's going to be taking it back on the target line.

DW: That will be taking it back on the target line, right, that visual, the target line. What we want to do is we want to see that more inward path, right, that we've been talking about, and we're going to go ahead and I'm going to make this backswing, keeping my left arm tight to my chest.

Drills

I want the Sweetspot to trace inward at the same rate the hands are basically. My wrists are going to be hinging as I do this of course. When I do this correctly, my left arm is going to miss those two sticks completely. Okay. And that sets me up as I push my Weight Forward for a perfect downswing Sweetspot Path.

CE: Okay. Good!

DW: Makes it real simple, as long as you get this in there correctly --

CE: Right.

DW: -- pretty, pretty easy job there to do, and then once it's set up right, it makes it real easy to be sure, not only the Sweetspot, but the hands are going back on the proper path.

CE: So let's say you go ahead and take it back on the proper path at the top.

DW: Okay.

CE: But you're one of those players that now feel like you have to, instead of move the lower body, move the upper body.

DW: Yeah.

CE: So you would come

out this way, and you would automatically feel that.

DW: I'm going to crash right into it, right?

CE: You're going to crash.

DW: And my Sweetspot is nowhere near the proper path in that regard.

CE: But if you got there and then you did of course our Weight Forward.

DW: Yeah.

CE: And you drag it forward. This is going to come right back down that path again.

DW: No problem whatsoever.

CE: It's going to miss that right there.

DW: Right on through.

CE: You get it, right. Great! That's a great drill!

CE: All right, so now what we're going to do is we're going to take this part and show you another drill for Sweetspot Path. So we'll lay this club down as a target line, let's say, and now I'm going to grab a two by four.

DW: Okay.

CE: And we're going to put that along the Sweetspot Path. Now, the distance from this board to this ball is going to depend on what club you have. So if you have wedges and short irons, well, a wedge is, primarily is going to be about 6 inches and the short irons, 7, 8, 9, are going to be about 8 inches from the back of the board to the ball. So as I get set I want to make sure I do two things; that I miss the board going back and that I miss the board coming down. So if I move over into my right hip and

Drills

I sway my upper body, I'm going to hit the board. So what I want to do is stretch out my right side, get my left shoulder going downward as the path goes up, and as I move the Weight Forward, the club is going to come right back down the two by four, on that path, strike the ball, and then exit through. So again, if I hang back on my back foot, I'm going to hit the board. If I get here and I start moving the clubhead past my hands, I'm going to hit the board. So in just a little swing, I'm just going to make one little swing, what I want to do is make sure that I miss this going back and down.

DW: Beautiful!

CE: And that's going to allow me to get the Sweetspot moving on the right path, which is going to help with the Flat Left Wrist. So if you're hearing that sound, this sound, [knocking sound] stop! Okay? Do it again until you don't hear that sound.

DW: And if you're hearing that beautiful sound of ball and divot --

CE: Keep going.

DW: -- you've got something going. If I can ask here too, this is angled pretty fair amount in from that target line. We're not putting that straight on the target line, this is at about a --

CE: 10-11 degrees.

DW: Okay.

CE: So what we don't want is we don't want to feel like we're going this way along the target line, because it would go outside there, right?

DW: Right!

CE: By the same token, we just don't want to jerk our hands inside, all right, so it's a controlled motion of everything starting to move back with the Sweetspot going on top of that line, all the way to the top, and then it's coming right back down that line again into the golf ball, and then it just exits right out.

DW: Looks great! Looks pretty easy there!

CE: Yeah, that's a pretty simple drill, and everybody has old two by fours laying around in their garage.

DW: Yeah. Right!

Clubface Control Drills

CE: All right Dave, let's talk a little bit now about Clubface Control, because ultimately, at the end of the day, you have to control it as a golf ball.

Drills

DW: That's right.

CE: And what's going to control that is that clubface relative to the path, which means you have to educate your hands on what they need to do.

DW: ...How to control that, yeah.

CE: So go ahead and show us a couple of things.

DW: I'll go ahead and take my setup here and I'm going to do it right on this, what we've set down sort of as a target line there. And it's white so it's nice to see on here, but if I go ahead and make some mini little backswings, I'm going to go ahead and actually stop right down here at what would be impact, okay, and I'm basically, as I do this and I work on this, and I train myself, I'm going to train myself to return a square clubface.

CE: Right!

DW: An open clubface, or even possibly a closed clubface. And I want to learn what the difference is, what that feels like, what that feels like in my hands, because again, it's all about educating these hands. We want to know what that's all about, what that feeling is all about. So I can actually go ahead and set up, put myself in an impact position, push the handle forward with the Flat Left Wrist in place, with the Weight Forward, and I can go ahead and feel the difference here. I'm going to go square, open, closed.

CE: Right!

DW: Okay? So I want to be able to feel the differences in those positions.

Purestrike

Now, I can go ahead if I was going to do this and almost kind of use the ground to help me kind of stop this in a little drill, I could go ahead and I can make some swings, stopping sort of down here with a square clubface.

CE: Right!

DW: Stopping with a little bit more of an open clubface. Stopping with a little bit more of a closed clubface.

CE: Right!

DW: Just in training those and I can chip some balls doing that too.

CE: Right!

DW: And sort of hit the ball and stop just past impact and sort of check that face.

CE: Right! So you can check it here, and you could also check it by doing a little drill on the through side.

DW: Yeah, yeah, I can go ahead and I can do little follow-through drills here and I can check to see if it's either, right, in more of a toe-up position.

CE: Right!

DW: Okay? I might make the ball -- I might make the trajectory of the ball fly a little lower. Little lower,

CE: but no curve necessarily.

DW: No curve. I could make the ball be more of a standard trajectory here, a little more angled on the line, right, and I can go what feels like, almost like --

Drills

CE: Clubface facing the sky.

DW: Yeah, clubface is just facing the sky, like I almost put a glass of water on that thing.

CE: Right!

DW: Right? And that would make -- that would be the highest trajectory.

CE: The highest trajectory.

DW: Yeah.

CE: So all of those three, the only thing they really do is perform trajectory.

DW: Absolutely!

CE: And the curvature has nothing to do with which motion you're using, that's just changes trajectory amount. So a curvature is based on what that face relationship is to the path when the ball is leaving.

DW: All the way, face relationship to path, that's a big thing to remember.

CE: Well, so we've got an orange stick set up out here.

DW: Okay.

CE: So if you want to work on starting location of your golf ball and/or curve, you could first maybe hit shots to the right of the stick, and if they start right and continue to go right, or start right and stay right, then you know you'd have to close your path just a little, or close your face just a little on that path.

DW: Right, to match that path.

CE: And then we might want to start them left and then adjust the face as well.

DW: Right, with the clubface pointing left, it will start left; the clubface pointing right, it will start right.

CE: Right! And then the final one is you'd actually hit the stick.

DW: Try drill it right into it.

CE: Good luck with that!

Drills

DW: So if I'm going to do this, I'm going through kind of the feelings I've had, I've been educating my hands. I'm going to start by just going ahead and chip a couple of balls here. First one, I'm going to go ahead and I'm going to chip this to the right of the stick. Okay? Okay. Beautiful! Just pushed out to the right of the stick. This next one I'm going to go ahead again, working on educating my hands in that Clubface Control, same alignments. I'm going to chip this to the left of the stick. Okay? Now let's see if we can get one to go straight at that stick. Pretty much right over it.

CE: So that's how you'd work on controlling the face, little bit open, little bit close, little bit square, and that's going to show you these starting directions.

DW: Right, practicing with those starting lines.

CE: Yeah, so again, this is something you can do in your backyard with some of those foam golf balls even.

DW: Right, right!

CE: You know, just take a stick back and go at it.

DW: Yeah, you don't need to be out at your range, you can do this anywhere.

CE: Yeah, that's a couple of really good drills to learn Clubface Control.

DW: Yeah, it's simple to work on.

CE: Yeah! All righty!

PureStrike: Lessons

DAVE WEDZIK: Okay, for the most part what we want you to pay attention to is what your head is going to do during the swing.

LORI: Okay.

DW: Because one of the keys we teach around is a Steady Head. Okay? And how that staying steady makes everything a little more consistent, okay? So really going to notice just how much it goes way down at the backswing. Okay? At the same time, one of the things that's making it go down, one of the things you're not doing, let's say, that's making you go down, gives you about I'd say, what would you say, Chuck, about a 70 degree shoulder turn maybe? Maybe 60 or 70, so you're losing some power there --

LORI: Okay.

DW: -- by not turning your shoulders all the way. Then the other thing is, you've got to hope you kind of can raise it back up. So there's like a...

LORI: Yes...

DW: ...there's a lot of compensation that's going to go on in there, okay? So I think what's going to help you the most as a golfer getting started, would be to explain to you how you keep your head steady.

LORI: Uh-huh.

DW: Right? Simple as that.

110

Lessons

CHUCK EVANS: If you start at five-four.

LORI: Five, exactly, on a good day.

[Laughter]

CE: And you go down to five-one. If you stayed there, that club becomes like 4 inches longer, right?

LORI: Right, right!

CE: So you get behind the golf ball. Well, so we realize that, so now we go up this way. Well, if I started here at five-four, but I go up this way to five-seven, now the club's also 3 inches shorter.

LORI: Uh-huh.

CE: All right! So we've got to try to keep that level of the head.

LORI: Yes, and I see it. I mean, I do sit and watch people swing a lot, because we live close to the range.

DW: Okay.

LORI: And I see how they swing and I watch, and I mean, now watching myself for the first time I realize like how I do look much different.

DW: Well, and a lot of their heads are moving around a little bit too. We see a lot of this, so.

LORI: Right, right!

DW: So let's talk about how we fix that up and the nice little bonus out of this is, as we do this we're going to increase your shoulder turn and we should start to hit the ball a little further too.

LORI: Okay. That's a good thing.

Purestrike

DW: If we start it out and just try to explain to you, let's talk about what makes your head go down.

LORI: Okay.

DW: And then what is the sort of controlling piece that would stop it from going down so much. So if you go ahead and take your setup here.

LORI: Okay.

DW: Okay? And you notice you're kind of forward bent from the hips, right, you're a little bit bent over. Now, as you start your backswing, if you stay kind of forward bent and your left shoulder is going down like this --

LORI: Right.

DW: -- that would make your head go down.

LORI: Right, yes.

DW: Okay? And limit your shoulder turn at the same time. All right? The controlling thing to keeping your head stable in this case for you is actually to understand that even though your left shoulder is going down --

LORI: Right!

DW: -- and you're bending this way a little bit, you're also sort of extending or almost having the feeling of standing up. You're kind of stretching out this way, and almost feeling like your, you know, head is almost -- for you, it's going to feel like your head might be rising up a little.

LORI: Right, right, right!

DW: Chuck will kind of demonstrate.

CE: Right! So in this angle it would look, if you're here, it's going to feel

Lessons

like you're stretching this whole side up that way.

LORI: Okay.

CE: This way, I mean, just like pulling a tight thing.

LORI: Yeah.

CE: As you're doing that, your left shoulder is starting to go down a little bit. You see, those two combinations is what keeps my head steady.

LORI: Uh-huh.

CE: If all I did was stretch, but I didn't move my shoulders down, I'd pull straight up.

LORI: Right.

CE: If I just move my shoulder down --

DW: Without any of that stretching up.

CE: Without any of this, my head goes down.

LORI: Okay.

CE: So this is going to stretch upward while the left shoulder is moving downward.

LORI: Downward, okay.

CE: And then as you come into the ball, you do the very same thing on the other side, so you stretch the left side.

LORI: Stretch out, okay.

DW: So go ahead and setup.

PureStrike

LORI: Okay.

DW: And you're going to feel like you take this back hip right up this whole side, as you do your backswing, you keep stretching it and keep raising it up.

LORI: What about this arm?

DW: That's all right. We're not going to worry too much about right there. That's pretty much going to stay in place. It's not going to do anything much different than its bend doing for you. Okay? But your big thing is, you're just going to keep feeling like you keep stretching up, right? You keep feeling like -- you feel much straighter, your back feels now. Rather than you were kind of like this before, right?

LORI: Right, yeah, I was coming through like with my arms.

DW: Yeah. I know what you're saying. So you're going to feel like you're really stretching out. Your whole back is kind of straightening as you stretch that right hip up in the air.

LORI: Okay.

DW: So let's try that again.

CE: Let's do it in slow motion.

LORI: Okay.

CE: All right! So stretch the right side.

DW: There you go. Feel how much stretch you feel right in there.

Lessons

LORI: Yes, totally different feeling.

CE: And so now you have, you know, 90 degrees or more of shoulder turn.

LORI: Right! Oh, I can feel it, even in my shoulder and everything.

CE: Yes.

DW: Enormous shoulder turn, that's good.

LORI: Okay.

CE: Okay. So let's do that in a swing at about 50% speed.

LORI: Okay.

CE: Okay?

DW: Now, we're in the driver, we're not going to go slamming it full board here. I'm going to move, I'm going to move. I'm going to give you this feeling one more time. What I'd like to do for you actually is I'm going to take the club from you and do one other thing.

LORI: Okay.

DW: So I want you to go ahead and bend over with your arms forward like you were at address.

LORI: Uh-huh.

DW: I want to isolate this feeling of the back like kind of stretching and extending, okay? So it would be like, I'm going to give it to you two ways. Here we go, ready? You just try to isolate it, ready?

LORI: Okay.

DW: Ooh! There's that like stretching out.

Purestrike

LORI: Right!

DW: Okay? But as soon as you start turning, as you do that same things, now you just feel like stretching out, there you go. There's what we're talking about.

LORI: I feel it, yes.

DW: Really stretching out. So if I was to isolate it, that stretching out would look like that. Just keep stretching out like that. There we go. Okay?

LORI: Okay.

CE: And let's see, and again, do it at about 50% speed.

LORI: Okay.

DW: Okay? So you're just going to keep stretching up, up, up, keep stretching, keep extending, beautiful! And a draw.

LORI: Holy Moses!

Lessons

DW: Did you see a draw?

LORI: Yeah. All right! That was too good!

DW: That was awesome right there.

LORI: It felt good. I didn't even swing that hard.

DW: You don't draw them all the time?

LORI: No!

DW: Push that handle forward, there you go, all right, whenever you're ready. Wow! Look at it.

CE: Little draw!

DW: Another draw! Another draw! Take a look at the difference here. Look at how -- look at that backswing? Look at how big that shoulder turn is.

LORI: Yes. It's almost beyond my face, yeah.

DW: So that's going to create some power right there, beautiful! Good extension on that follow-through too.

CE: Yeah.

DW: Very nice! Very nice!

CE: So that's one of what we call keys.

Purestrike

LORI: Okay.

CE: You know, you want to keep your head steady.

LORI: Uh-huh.

CE: We have five of them, but that particular one is the one you need to do right now to stop all this stuff.

LORI: And it's a different feel. I mean, it feels better.

DW: Yeah.

CE: Yeah. It should feel tighter, should feel more powerful.

LORI: It does. And I don't even feel like I'm swinging even as hard, but I see the distance, you know?

CE: Right, right! Good!

DW: What's really-- how great is it in the midst of keeping your head steady by doing it the right way, you get the increased shoulder turn to get more power.

LORI: It's a good thing. I like it.

DW: Great!

CE: All right! Thank you!

DW: Thank you! Very good! Very good!

DW: What we're going to do is we're going to ask you just to go ahead, and as you normally would, hit a few shots. I'm going to shoot a little video here of your swing, and we're going to take a look at it together. Okay?

Lessons

ALEX: Okay.

CE: What is your typical miss, what's the problem that you have more than anything?

ALEX: I come behind the ball.

CE: So you hit a little fat?

ALEX: Yeah, sometimes.

CE: Go ahead and hit a few shots.

DW: All right! So --

CE: Oh, there is the fat shot.

DW: Yeah, and I think that's pretty interesting, right? We saw some thin shots and we saw some fat shots, right?

CE: Right!

DW: So I'm going to step up here with the camera. You can see actually pretty Steady Head, pretty nice backswing here, right? This is all looking pretty good, you're in a pretty good place to work from here. It looks to me, as this comes down, you can see how that forearm and shaft get in line really early there, right? It looks to me like you're almost trying to like scoop this ball or help it up in the air. You have the feeling sometimes like you're almost trying to --

Purestrike

ALEX: Yeah.

DW: you know, get the ball in the air a little bit, okay, and that actually with that left wrist bending like this so much, you can see how that left forearm -- Chuck will demonstrate that for you real quick with that left forearm and the shaft getting out of line. See, how bent the left wrist is there?

ALEX: Uh-huh.

DW: That's destroying this radius here and it's also -- it's making it really difficult to hit the ball in the air, actually even though it feels like you'd want to -- you could get it in the air, because as that left wrist gets bent, you can see how you're either going to hit the ball back -- hit the ground behind the ball, or you'd hit the ball with this leading edge sometimes and hit them. Right? That sole of the club isn't down there on the ground, so Chuck would demonstrate doing this correctly for you.

CE: So now what would happen is you'd move your Weight Forward, but you'd also keep moving your hands forward, so your hands would actually be past the golf ball before the clubhead ever hits it. If you look at the bottom of your club here, where I just noticed this, you'll see that your grass marks are not even to the first groove.

ALEX: Yeah.

CE: All right! So that means the club is going this way all the time. You're getting everything thin, unless you hit it fat, all right? So the feeling of impact is your weight should be forward, so your Weight Forward and your hands are forward.

DW: There we go.

CE: That's impact up here.

120

Lessons

DW: There we go.

CE: Okay?

DW: So it should be -- it should be almost the opposite of trying to lift the ball in the air. It should feel like you're actually trying to --

CE: Hitting the ground.

DW: -- and essentially deal off the club. Almost like you're going to feel like you're going to compress the ball down. Okay?

ALEX: All right!

DW: And so first part of this is just exactly what Chuck was doing there, showing you what really impact is, what it's supposed to feel like. You want to show us again what impact kind of should look like?

CE: Yeah. So go ahead and bring it forward. More. There you go.

DW: Now, you see how flat your left wrist is there.

CE: See, this is flat now.

DW: Okay.

CE: Back here it's bent, isn't it?

ALEX: Yeah.

CE: So see the difference where the club's pointing?

ALEX: Uh-huh.

CE: So this is what club, 7-iron?

ALEX: Yes.

CE: All right! So now it's a 9, and now it's a 5.

DW: Now, where does that look like your hands are to your foot? How far forward does that look like your hands are, say, in relation to your foot?

ALEX: They're like even.

CE: If you kept your head right here, it looks like it's over the top of your left foot?

ALEX: Yeah.

CE: Okay, that's your impact location.

DW: Yeah, that's where we're trying to get to.

CE: See, your arms hanging in a straight line over here now, instead of aligned back in there, see that? So you're moving everything left including your hands. So you don't stop for the ball, we don't want to try to help it in the air, we're actually trying to hit downward on that direction. Okay?

Lessons

DW: Okay. It's good.

CE: All right! So here's what we're going to do. I'll put this board back here like this.

ALEX: Uh-huh

CE: All right? So now when you take it back, you're going to miss this board, and you bring it down, you're going to miss the board. If you do this, you're going to hit the board. [knocking sound] So you don't want to hear that sound we just heard, okay?

DW: Chip it out to the end of the tee, handle forward, I want you to feel like these hips stay forward throughout. Okay, that's going to help keep that left wrist flat. I'm just going to keep everything finishing up to here. There you go. Okay. Chip it to the end of the tee. Beautiful!

CE: There you go.

DW: Beautiful! Beautiful job!

CE: Good job! So where are you looking at right now, Alex, when you're looking down here, where are you looking?

ALEX: Right here.

CE: Okay. So keep your eyes focused up here. So you're trying to -- what

PureStrike

you're trying to do is hit a spot up here with your club, okay?

DW: Let the ball get in the way. The handle forward, hips forward, chip it off to the end of the tee. Beautiful!

CE: There you go. Much better!

DW: Beautiful!

CE: There you go.

DW: Very good!

CE: Good! Good! Good! Good!

DW: Remember that sensation right there --

CE: And that sound.

DW: -- that's the feeling.

CE: It has a sound, it has the feeling.

ALEX: All right!

DW: Good job!

CE: Good job dude!

DW: Good job!

Lessons

DW: What problems do you generally have? Do you have any problems that, you know, are glaring for you?

JEFF: Hitting it thin, hitting it fat, and you know not --

DW: Okay.

JEFF: -- getting a divot where you're supposed to --

DW: Okay, so contact issues, divot not in front of the ball --

JEFF: Yeah, consistency. Sure!

DW: Some typical problems. What's your handicap?

JEFF: About a ten-and-a-half.

DW: Okay, okay.

CE: And which ways you miss typically, when you miss, you miss right or left?

JEFF: Sometimes I'll hook it.

CE: Okay.

JEFF: If I don't hit it just right off, you know, kind of turn too much.

DW: Okay.

CE: Well, go ahead and hit some shots we'll take a little video. We'll look at the video and we'll see where we're going to start.

JEFF: Perfect!

DW: Pretty decent there.

DW: Okay, so it was a little thin, right?

JEFF: Yeah.

DW: So I mean, you're a ten, so you're going to hit some balls solid, you're going to take some divots in the right place. To start with, one of the big keys to hitting the ball solidly and putting the divot in front of the golf ball would be having a Flat Left Wrist. So easy way to attain that or

Lessons

start with would be putting a little bit more Weight Forward at address and setting up with the left wrist a little bit flatter, so it puts the hand a little bit more forward. But the biggest thing is we're trying to swing around a Steady Head, right, to stay a little more centered on the golf ball, and you can see how much up into the right --

JEFF: Yes.

DW: -- your head is going there.

JEFF: Yeah.

DW: So we want to start there, we're going to talk about how you get a Steady Head and how that helps and how some of these changes we make, how that will actually help with your weight being a little more forward and keeping your left wrist a little flatter and doing some of those things.

CE: So let's go ahead and set up like you were. So as you set up, like we saw in the video, you've got a little bit of bend in this wrist. In other words, the back of this hand is not aligned with this wrist.

JEFF: Okay.

CE: So let's push this forward just a touch. So now we've got a little flatter angle right there.

DW: So a little closer, little closer would impact you. You know what, let's do one other quick thing here. Jeff, I'd like you -- so you show me what your address position is again, okay? And I'd like you to actually show us your image of what impact should like is.

CE: Yeah, just so --

DW: I'd like you to show us what you think impact looks like.

JEFF: Really like that.

DW: Okay. That's pretty good. We would say it even looks a little more.

CE: This way.

DW: And a little more Weight Forward. Okay? So we start there by just getting -- I want you to understand where impact is and what it really looks like, what it really feels like.

CE: Yeah, the difference between address and impact, because they're not the same, unless you already started at impact position, right? So go ahead and do that again, so you go address, now go impact. Hand forward, Weight Forward, there you go. Perfect! Perfect!

JEFF: Okay.

CE: So knowing where you're trying to get to, you know, is a big part of solving this puzzle really.

JEFF: Yeah.

DW: I mean, it's -- you know, that would help.

JEFF: Yeah.

DW: So go ahead back to your setup. We'll have -- Chuck is going to go through that little setup change there, we talked about that, while we flatten out that left wrist.

CE: Now we're going to flatten this out at address, so now as you start back what you want to feel like is that you're going to stretch the whole right side of your body out, like it's one big stretch base.

Lessons

DW: This whole side.

CE: And to do that you're stretching it out and your left shoulder feels like it's going towards your left knee.

DW: Yeah. And you stretch that almost like you're feeling this whole seam of your shirt go almost towards the target.

CE: You're seeing it stretched up here like this? That's what it's going to feel like. And now from here, when you start to downswing, your heads -- your hips are going to push forward, not turn; push, yeah. Now, see your hips are turned.

JEFF: Oh!

CE: Yeah, there you go.

JEFF: Okay.

DW: You're just going to let the weight keep pushing just a little more forward.

CE: Now, after contact you can go ahead and turn. All right! But if you turn too quick, it's going to throw the club out too quick.

JEFF: Right!

CE: All right? So let's go through that again. So you've got your Steady Head, you're going to stretch out your right side.

DW: Stretching, stretching, stretching, stretching.

CE: There you go.

PureStrike

DW: And you're just going to shift that Weight Forward to that impact position.

CE: Now get the hands to impact. There you go. And now you can turn right out of it.

DW: And a lot of times I know, Chuck, you'll do this too I'm sure, a lot of times what we do with the students is, we might ask you to feel an exaggeration. So in this case, you might actually have to feel like you're stretching this so much towards the target, right, it's putting in so much bend, that your head's actually going forward. We know your head's going backing up this much, it would be okay to feel like your head actually goes down and forward as you do this.

JEFF: Okay.

CE: So that would feel like this, Jeff, go ahead and start it back.

DW: Yeah, that would be the feeling.

CE: That would be the feeling.

DW: Yeah, right. You won't actually attain that. Let's see a backswing where you feel like you do it that much, if you hit this ball.

Lessons

DW: Beautiful job! Beautiful! Let's see a backswing where you feel like you move your head down and forward even more as you stretch.

DW: Beautiful.

CE: There you go.

DW: Now, let's see you do -- let's see you just do just a basic pitch with that sensation, just chip the ball.

DW: Beautiful job! Beautiful job!

CE: Much better divot.

PureStrike

DW: How about the depth of that divot?

CE: How about that one?

DW: Can you believe the depth of that divot?

CE: Very nice job.

DW: You said you couldn't take divot.

JEFF: Never seen those before.

DW: That must be the deepest divot you have ever seen. Beautiful job!

CE: That's a deep divot.

DW: In doing that stretch, how much did it feel like your head actually had to go down and forward?

JEFF: It's a feeling I've never had before. Like I was almost going to fall that way.

CE: Right, but the video will show you that it just stayed in line. Now let's look at the video.

Lessons

DW: All right, see all that extension, now you've got all that stretching on that side of your body, okay? Beautiful job!

CE: Now the hips start to --

JEFF: Oh yeah.

DW: And look at the difference. Everything is forward, that shaft is leaning more forward.

JEFF: Doesn't even look like me.

DW: There you go. Beautiful job!

JEFF: Thank you!

DW: So you've been working on you said not coming over the top so much and trying to approach the ball more from the inside.

CHRIS: Trying to get to the inside of the ball.

DW: This is key #4 for us is, you know, understanding and controlling the Sweetspot Path. So I want you to notice a couple of things here. The Sweetspot Path starts on the backswing, right?

CE: Yeah.

DW: And you're doing a nice job with that early in the backswing, but it continues going back up and inwards--

CE: So it keeps going this way and you do pretty good right in here and then you start going vertical with it.

CHRIS: Okay.

PureStrike

DW: And that's where your head starts going up a little bit as well, but you're going to see you start lifting your arms --

CE: So there is a lot of lift right there.

DW: --all the way to the top, okay, so that whole -- the completion of the backswing was -- just kept lifting, lifting, lifting, lifting, lifting your arms, okay?

CHRIS: Uh-huh.

DW: And as you start doing that, that's the first -- that's the first part, that's the start of when you're going to start coming right over the top. Okay? So I would say as much of work as you've done, I'm sure you've improved this, all right, and you've improved a lot this summer, and I think a lot of it's been too just from hitting -- going and hitting a lot of golf balls too, and getting a lot of practice in.

CE: Now, see how the shaft is coming out, around your neck up there?

CHRIS: Okay, so it should be back here more?

DW: It should be right there, just underneath the shoulder.

CHRIS: Oh wow!

DW: Okay. And you're going to see how much this club has been -- you can see that shaft --

CE: You can see how the club's out, and the shaft's in.

CHRIS: All right!

DW: So if we were to lay down a --

Lessons

CE: We'll lay down the tracks. All right! So this is going to represent your target line, Chris.

CHRIS: Okay.

CE: And this is going to represent what we call your Sweetspot line, in other words, what the club actually travels on. So in the backswing we want you to feel like, if you go ahead and set up to that, we want you to feel like it's traveling on this line, but it continues to travel on this line back up and in this direction, okay?

DW: Your hands keep driving back behind that right shoulder; your hands keep driving inward. They control the Sweetspot for the most part there, so --

CE: Yeah, so from there, let's go to the top right there, and so you're going to feel the hands more in, and from here you're going to feel the hips slide forward, slide, yeah, and then move this Sweetspot right down that line to the golf ball and then come back leftward.

CHRIS: So you want to slide in there, not to trap --

CE: Absolutely! Because the slide is what's going to help you get the club to stay back, if you have any turn, that's what throws the club out.

CHRIS: Okay.

CE: So we want to slide in to impact.

CHRIS: All right!

DW: So let's take that up to the top again done properly, with not only the Sweetspot, but the hands controlling the Sweetspot, working inward, they keep working inward, keep working inward, okay? Now, as the weight starts going forward and the hips slide, see how that --

CE: See how the club is back here now.

CHRIS: Oh yeah.

DW: Okay? So your visual of the down stroke ends up being that the club is approaching very much on this type of an angle.

CHRIS: All right!

DW: Now, I'm going to add one other thing here to kind of help you with this, say this -- the slide portion, okay, and what I'd like to do is, if you go ahead and take your setup, okay, what I would suggest here is Weight Forward is a big key and that's why we're sliding, to keep the Weight Forward, to keep the club approaching from the inside. So we're going to feel like the weight stays forward throughout the backswing, okay, as the hands in the Sweetspot trace in. And you can even feel like what Chuck is going to do right there is he's going to actually do it real slow, I want you to feel like all your weight stays -- there we go.

CE: You're going to feel like you stay right on this hip.

DW: There we go, as your hands go inward. We want to just keep it more centered, so for you that's going to feel like it starts a little more forward and actually stays more forward through the backstroke, there we go. There you go. So it's going to be weight more forward throughout with the Sweetspot and the hands more inward, tracing that inclined plan.

CE: Going to get set there for a second and keep the weight left.

DW: You're going to keep that weight as much forward.

Lessons

CE: So you want to feel this is into the backswing right here.

CHRIS: Okay.

CE: Or just the sole stroke.

DW: See how much your left arm is inward, there we go. Left arm way inward, hips forward. Beautiful job!

CE: There you go.

DW: Beautiful job!

CE: Good!

DW: I'm going to step in and grab this camera, I'd like to have a video of this.

CE: Now, I'm going to put this club right here.

CHRIS: Uh-huh.

CE: Now, your job is to miss this club going back and miss it coming down. There we go.

PureStrike

DW: There you go. Look at the difference here, look how much inward those hands are. Wait til you see this? Oh my goodness. Now look where the shaft is coming up. See, how that's right through the bicep? Beautiful! Watch this, tracing the Sweetspot Path the whole way down.

CHRIS: All right!

DW: Outstanding!

CE: See, originally your shaft is coming out through the neck in the downswing, now ---

CHRIS: you want it down here.

CE: Yeah.

CHRIS: All right!